the GRACE TREE

A Journey into Freedom

DEAN MAERZ

Copyright © 2014 by Dean Maerz

First Edition – 2014

ISBN

978-1-4602-4809-6 (Hardcover)

978-1-4602-4810-2 (Paperback)

978-1-4602-4811-9 (eBook)

Unless otherwise identified, Scripture quotations are taken from the New American Standard Bible®, Copyright © 1960, 1962, 1963, 1968, 1971, 1972, 1973, 1975, 1977, 1995 by The Lockman Foundation. Used by permission.

Scripture quotations marked NKJV are taken from the New King James Version. Copyright © 1979, 1980, 1982 by Thomas Nelson, Inc. Used by permission. All rights reserved.

Scripture quotations marked ESV are taken from The Holy Bible, English Standard Version® (ESV®), copyright © 2001 by Crossway. Used by permission. All rights reserved.

Scripture quotations marked NIV are taken from the *Holy Bible, New International Version*®. Copyright © 1973, 1978, 1984 by International Bible Society. Used by permission of Zondervan. All rights reserved.

Scripture quotations marked JBP are taken from the New Testament in Modern English, translated by J. B. Phillips. Copyright © 1947, 1952, 1955, 1957, 1958 by the Macmillan Company, New York. Used by permission. All rights reserved.

Scripture quotations marked KJV are taken from the King James Version.

All emphasis within Scripture quotations is the author's own.

Produced by:

FriesenPress

Suite 300 - 990 Fort St

Victoria, BC, Canada, V8V 3K2

www.friesenpress.com

Distributed to the trade by The Ingram Book Company

TABLE OF CONTENTS

Acknowledgements

I would like to thank Adria Vizzi Holub for your unique role in editing this manuscript. Your scholarly attention to detail, theological expertise, and listening heart were invaluable and vital to the final outcome. Thanks for your honesty, all of the amusing editing comments, and all of the brilliant, selfless ideas. The "white dove" in front of my truck was definitely spot-on.

I would also like to thank Sylvia Buchholz for your trusted input, double-duty proofing, and patiently letting me bounce these ideas off of you over the past few years on a weekly basis. You are, in part, responsible for this book being written—more than you know.

To my dear wife, Adeline, thanks for your support and your honest, "no holds barred," chopping and proofing skills. Honey, you are one of a kind, and the very best!

Thanks to Jasmine Wiebe, Bonnie Schmunk, and Laurie Vankleek for additional proofing, and Charlene Witt for the title idea.

Thanks to Laura Patricia Hernandez and Arielle Ratzlaff for the cover image.

I would also like to thank all of the people who have encouraged me to write over the past few years: those in our Monday night Bible study, friends, family, and acquaintances. I would not have taken this project on had you not persistently urged me to consider it. In the end, I have discovered a brand new medium of expression, but I must warn you, it is extremely addictive, and I may be pestering you with new manuscript ideas soon.

I would also like to mention my dear Grandma Jacobson, who at age 98, has just recently gone home to eternity. Thank you for your support and love through the years—I can feel you cheering me on from the other side.

Last, but definitely not least, I would like to acknowledge an extravagantly gracious Jesus. Without Your grace, I am quite sure I wouldn't be alive right now; words cannot express my gratitude. Thank you so much.

Foreword

You must not miss the compelling and delightful multi-layered journey described in Dean Maerz's "the Grace Tree." I love the folksy anecdotes and illustrations taken from his personal journey through angst, to security in God's amazing grace. The pilgrimage from Eden to the New Jerusalem takes us down old pathways in a fresh new way. Also featured, is the centrality of grace in God's redemptive plan as revealed in the Scriptures. "The Grace Tree" has inspired me to be easier on both myself and others, and more passionate about personally embracing the available flow of amazing grace in my every day direction. Revival, here I come!

Fred Fulford,
Pastoral Theology Program Director
Summit Pacific College

Dedication

I would like to dedicate this book to all of those hungering for an "outpouring of grace." There has been much opposition and ridicule, but the small, unassuming seeds are being watered, and the streams of grace are dividing, widening, and deepening; stirring up hope and bringing life to everything they touch. There is no other way to be free apart from the pathways of grace. As for me, my chips are all in on this one; I have no back-up plan, it is all or nothing. And so, to the dear ones in my life who daily live out and exemplify the extravagantly free lifestyle of grace: this is for you.

Preface

A couple of years ago I decided to go to a conference. This is not an unusual thing for me; however, I was in one of those odd seasons in life when a particular subject kept coming up. It seemed every time I turned around, someone was talking about grace. Since I could not get away from it, I determined to find a meeting along this theme. Eventually I found an "outside of the box" conference just down the coast from where I live, so I signed up.

Once there, I could tell this wasn't going to be an ordinary weekend. Thirty minutes into the first night so many of my religious paradigms were on the verge of collapse that my heart and my brain were overloaded. I went back to the hotel swimming with thoughts and emotions. By the end of the weekend I had more to think about and sort through than I ever imagined possible.

The next week, back at home, I began the process of breaking down and assimilating what I had heard. I knew that in order for me to embrace such a major shift in thinking, I had to have more than a concept; I had to have an encounter. I also had to have more than an isolated idea found somewhere in the Bible; it had to flow in context from the beginning of Genesis to the last verse of Revelation. For this reason I was drawn to the book of Genesis to start the rebuilding process. I didn't understand the new paradigm all at once—it took a lot of time and patience to sort through, and I spent many late nights on my knees asking the Holy Spirit for keys to certain questions that were perplexing me.

The contents of this book are a result of nearly two years of searching, learning, meditating, and sitting in the presence of Jesus. I can honestly say this process has taken my entire view of God, disassembled it, and then reconstructed it. It has been an interesting couple of years.

I was talking with my dad a month or two after I started on this writing project and he gave me a well-suited illustration that mirrored what I had been going through. My father, being the quintessential farm boy, told me of a time when he and his brothers had to clear the rocks from several acres of unbroken pasture land. He said, "Dean, as you write you will be digging up rocks. Some of them will be small, some large, and some you will have to move with a crowbar; but under each rock there will be a surprise. Some of them will have interesting little creatures living under them; in fact beneath some you might find a whole world of activity. Sometimes you can't even find the big rocks until you move the smaller ones from the surface and even then it is impossible to tell their size until you just start digging."

And that is the way it has been. I started moving rocks and I have uncovered much hidden treasure in the process. In the end I encountered the God of grace and my heart has been transformed. It is my hope that as you come on this journey with me, the same will be true for you.

Here is to discovering uncharted territory together.

Dean

Chapter 1
The Beginning

I love beginnings. As long as I can remember, I have never tired of watching things happen for the first time. The process of new life, new direction, and new ways of thinking provide endless sources of amusement for me.

I have an unusual relationship with digital clocks and read-out devices, such as odometers. I will watch a clock for four or five minutes to see it turn over to midnight. When it finally happens, I will close my eyes for a moment so I can savor the 12:00:00 a little longer. It is times like these I thank the Lord for the gift of "after image" He has put in our eyes. This marks the beginning of a new day; to most a mundane occurrence, to me a monumental happening. And you don't want to be driving with me when an odometer changes over to a new cycle—I will literally stop the vehicle and take a picture of it if I can. In my mind, my car has somehow been given a fresh chance at life; old things passed away, all things made new. If only I could convince my mechanic of this reality!

I grew up in a farming community and remember the many beginnings I witnessed there. It was an endless wonder of lifecycle regeneration. There were always new chicks, lambs, colts, and calves in the spring. Some might not realize that a newborn calf has no teeth. After a few days of suckling at their mother, we would put our hands in their mouths while dipping their heads in a pail of milk, to get them used to drinking from a bucket. This has to rank as one of the strangest sensations on the planet, a calf trying to suck your hand while learning to drink. The farm cats were in the business of having several litters of kittens each year. We would search the farmyard over several times until we discovered under which granary "Missy" hid her newest batch. The baby kittens would have their eyes closed for a few days until they adjusted to their new life under the shed.

I remember watching the nests of the migratory farm songbirds. They would come early in the spring to start their yearly lifecycle. I was particularly interested in the barn swallows that built their mud nests in the rafters of my grandfather's big red barn. After they laid their eggs I would watch "Mr. and Mrs. Swallow" guard the homestead by swooping dangerously close to our heads every time we approached.

Eventually they would hatch, and in a few short weeks they would line up on the side of the nest until they learned to fly.

However, out of the new life I have witnessed, nothing compares to the birth of a human baby. Somehow spirit, life, and destiny all come together in one moment. A marker is set, making us realize we are destined to live a cycle of generational years. Many times I have been touched by the first few moments of a newly married bride and groom just after they say, "I do." Then there are calendar beginnings like New Year's or a new month. Monday is the beginning of a new week, and, as already mentioned, every morning is the start of a new day. There are also new seasons of life such as a graduation, new job, new location to live, or new friendships.

> *Out of the new life I have witnessed, nothing compares to the birth of a human baby. Somehow spirit, life, and destiny all come together in one moment.*

Bible Beginnings

It is due to this lifelong fascination with beginnings that I love the book of Genesis in the Bible. The word "genesis" actually means "beginning." The first few chapters of this action packed book are filled with clues to our evxistence as a human race. They tell of our makeup as a human species, and our connection to the world we live in. They also make clear the reasons behind many of our core human drives.

I will give an example of this. One of the first recorded tasks given to Adam by God, besides keeping the garden, was to name all of the animals. It is stunning that, to this day, we cannot stop with this obsession. Biology, or the scientific study of life, has taken this task to a truly intricate system of classification. We still search out new life forms on our planet (and beyond), and upon finding an unknown species of amoeba in a Brazilian swamp, proceed to analyze, classify, and name it. We just can't get away from naming the creatures, plants, and rocks of our planet. It is an integral part of our DNA as human beings; an idiosyncrasy our heavenly Father put in us right from the start.

These scriptures also indicate where we have come from and where we are going. They contain clues to our original purpose for being placed on this planet. They give many insights concerning the state we find ourselves in and how we arrived at the place we are today. They speak clearly of God's love for us, His reason for creating us, and how we rejected that love.

Genesis 1-7 is particularly interesting. In the very first verse of the Bible we already see a profound first alluded to: "In the beginning, God created" (Genesis 1:1).

Here we see the first attribute given to God: He was creative. Most of us would agree that God is love, or some other character quality like kind or good, but here it states that God was first creative. He was, in fact, so creative that He couldn't help but build the entire universe as we know it. Every stage that He finished would be marked by "and God saw that it was good." The goodness in His heart was bringing forth good things, and God was taking great pleasure in the new world that He was shaping. We eventually see the creation of our human species in God's image and likeness.

It is amazing to think of the first words to land on human ears, "be blessed." This blessing was an empowerment, needed to accomplish the next words that the first man heard, "be fruitful and multiply and fill the earth and subdue it and have dominion" (Genesis 1:28, ESV). We then see the first job (gardening), the first romance, the first sin, and the first clothes (perhaps we should call this the first fashion statement). After that we find the first human birth, the first

> *It is amazing to think of the first words to land on human ears, "be blessed."*

sacrifice, the first offering, and the first murder. Then there are the first cities, the first musical instruments, the first boat (Noah's ark), the first near-annihilation of the human race, and the first use of alcohol to drown our sorrows. The list of firsts goes on.

There is, however, one first that, in my estimation, trumps all others when it comes to discovering who we are as a species. This first is so basic to our makeup and motivation that when we fail to understand it, we find ourselves in a place of dangerous disadvantage. In Genesis 3, we see our first struggle and, consequently, our first major life-altering choice as a human race. Most would say this was a struggle against sin—a struggle not to eat fruit from a forbidden tree. However, a closer inspection of the intricacies of this struggle puts it in a much different light. It was actually a choice where to look, but it became a choice between a blessing and a curse, between freedom and slavery, and ultimately between life and death.

It is this choice that we are going to examine in the following pages. We will talk about its profound but simple origins, then trace its implications through the ages, from the beginning, to the flood, to Moses and the Law, and finally to the cross and the subsequent grace that was poured out on our fallen world. In it we will discover much about our makeup as human beings, and the core motivations that lead us on paths of discovery, life, and death. We will also see what God's original intent was for us, and how He has made a way for us to regain all that was lost.

Chapter 2
The Choice

The crowning moment of creation came when God made Adam and Eve. Everything up to this time was done in anticipation of this event. The whole universe held its breath as the spirit of life was breathed into God's new creation. This new species of being was made in His likeness and image; something never conceived of before. God then placed His new prototype in a garden environment. We are not told how big the garden was, but we can assume it was a manageable size for them to handle. God has always been a specialist in aesthetics and this garden was no exception. It is remarkable to note that the word "Eden" means "pleasure and delight." This garden was a haven of harmony with nature, an empowerment of blessing, dominion, and grace. It is the original environment we were created to live in—one of pure pleasure and delight, love, friendship with God, and innocence. There were beautiful rivers, animals, gold and precious stones, and all kinds of plants.

The first man and woman were no exception to the beauty that surrounded them. Consider the fact that all of the genetic material needed to propagate the human race was resident in their bodies, which included thousands of years of human reproduction and billions of people. Adam and Eve carried perfect genetic code in their earthly bodies, and they were, no doubt, stunning creatures to look at. But this is only part of the story. We can surmise from many passages in the Bible that they were also covered with the very glory of heaven, giving them in essence, glorified bodies. This seems to mirror the fact that in the resurrection we will once again have glorified bodies, completing the cycle of our redemption.

> *Adam and Eve carried perfect genetic code in their earthly bodies, and they were, no doubt, stunning creatures to look at.*

So also is the resurrection of the dead. It is sown a perishable body, it is raised an imperishable body; it is sown in dishonor, it is raised in glory; it is sown in weakness, it is raised in power. (1 Corinthians 15:42-43)

These thoughts, combined with an environment devoid of guilt or shame, give us a glimpse into the reasons why

Adam and Eve weren't conscious of being naked, because the glory covered them. We can only imagine how this glory must have made them look; beautiful, shimmering with rainbows of vibrant color as they walked and worked in the garden.

The Two Trees

In the second chapter of Genesis we are told in particular about the trees of the garden. There were many varieties, and these large plants were evidently very beautiful. This verity is the first thing we are told about them. It is remarkable that their aesthetic value is mentioned first, even above the fact that they were good for food. Then there were two special trees that grew in the garden:

> *Out of the ground the Lord God caused to grow every tree that is pleasing to the sight and good for food: the tree of life also in the midst of the garden, and the tree of the knowledge of good and evil.* (Genesis 2:9)

From this passage we know that the tree of life was in the middle of the garden, and later on in Genesis 3 we are also told this was the location of the tree of the knowledge of good and evil. These two trees are crucial.

First, let us talk about the tree of life. We see it referred to literally in two places in the Bible, Genesis and Revelation. There are also a few places in Proverbs where the tree of life is mentioned metaphorically. The tree was first seen in Genesis 2:9 as quoted earlier. Then in the third chapter of Genesis, after Adam and Eve had fallen, there is a second mention of the tree of life:

Then the Lord God said, "Behold, the man has become like one of Us, knowing good and evil; and now, he might stretch out his hand, and take also from the tree of life, and eat, and live forever." (Genesis 3:22)

After this, God drove humankind out of the garden and stationed the cherubim to guard the way to the tree of life.

It is interesting to think about the tree of life. Had Adam and Eve eaten from it first, things would certainly be very different for us on this planet. We know from this passage that eating from this tree would have caused them to live forever. Since every spirit is created eternal, we can assume that eating from the tree of life would have given this same eternal life to their bodies. It would have somehow integrated into their core in such a way that they would have had an unending existence in the presence of God. This is a thought that is mind blowing: a fruit, that when eaten (consumed and assimilated internally into their bodies), would give life to them in such a way they would become immortal.

Now, let us look at the other tree in the garden, the tree of the knowledge of good and evil. This is the tree from which Eve, and then Adam, chose to eat. The serpent was not lying to Eve when he said that if she ate from this tree she would be like God, knowing good from evil: this is exactly what happened (Genesis 3:22). However, he did lie to her when he told her she would not die. It is also interesting that part of the allure was "her eyes would be opened and she would be like God." We have had a longing right from the beginning for our eyes to be opened, for revelation, to know and be more like God. But, there was something in that tree which, when consumed, produced death. Knowledge was released by this fruit; to be specific, a knowledge of good and evil.

> *The serpent was not lying to Eve when he said that if she ate, she would be like God, knowing good from evil. However, he did lie to her when he told her she would not die.*

Let us now take a closer look at the choice that Adam and Eve made:

> *Now the serpent was more crafty than any beast of the field that the Lord God had made. And he said to the woman,*

"Indeed, has God said, You shall not eat from any tree of the garden?" The woman said to the serpent, "From the fruit of the trees of the garden we may eat; but from the fruit of the tree that is in the middle of the garden, God has said, You shall not eat from it or touch it, or you will die." The serpent said to the woman, "You shall not surely die! For God knows that in the day you eat from it your eyes will be opened, and you will be like God, knowing good from evil." When the woman saw that the tree was good for food, and that it was a delight to the eyes, and that the tree was desirable to make one wise, she took from its fruit and ate, and she gave also to her husband with her, and he ate. Then the eyes of both of them were opened, and they knew that they were naked; and they sewed fig leaves together and made themselves loin coverings. (Genesis 3:1-7)

Notice how many times the words "eyes," "saw," and "delight to the eyes" are used. This was a choice of where Adam and Eve focused their attention more than anything. The first thing Eve did was take a good look at the tree. On closer inspection she saw it appeared to be good for food, it was pretty to look at, and she could somehow discern that it would give some kind of additional wisdom. She then took, ate, and gave it to her husband. The passage claims he was right there with her and there is no record of him objecting in any way. Then, an interesting thing happened. Their "eyes" were opened, which is exactly what the serpent said would happen. The first thing they did was look at themselves. We can only speculate what might have happened here. One theory is that after they ate, the glory covering disappeared and they for the first time saw they were naked. This would seem to line up with a verse in Romans, which tells us when we sin it has an adverse effect on the glory: "For all have sinned and fall short of the glory of God." (Romans 3:23) At least one thing is clear: their eyes led them into the mess, and their eyes now realized a new reality—nakedness—or in other words, shame and guilt.

The Knowledge of Good and Evil

Now let us look at the tree of the knowledge of good and evil a bit more carefully. It is intriguing how having a working knowledge of good and evil would produce death. Good just seems good to me. I mean, wouldn't it be a good thing to know about good? After all, God is good and we have been created in Christ Jesus for good works. Good is at least positive, and a whole lot better than bad. And think for a moment about the knowledge of evil. If you knew about evil, you could then use this information to stay away from those naughty things and, well, possibly do good things instead. It seems to me like this tree would be highly desirable to eat from, not a tree that would produce death. But not only did it produce death, its fruit was eternal, reaching down through countless generations. This pain far surpassed anything the moment of eating could have comprehended in a thousand years.

There was disobedience in the act of eating itself and it happened in three stages: looking, taking, and eating. This disobedience is called Adam's "offense" or "transgression" in the Bible (Romans 5:14). It was bad enough to cause the beautiful blessing given to them by God to reverse and become a bitter curse that was released in the earth. Genesis 3:17 says that the ground became cursed because of them.

> *The earth became at such odds with humankind that it is now possible for a person, if left unprotected, to die of exposure to our environment.*

Everything in nature suddenly became self-defensive and self-serving. Before this point in time, Adam and Eve worked the ground with ease. Because there was no reason for the world to mistrust them, it yielded fruit without reservation and without "sweat of the brow" labor. You see, the ground knew that Adam and Eve would not take unfair advantage of it. Now the world would demand labor for everything that was derived from it, and thorns and thistles would grow as a self-protection mechanism. In fact, the earth became at such odds with humankind that it is now possible for a person, if left unprotected, to die of exposure to our environment. Also, from that moment, a sin-nature was passed on to every individual born on this planet. The double edge of this sword is the knowledge that was released to them—an intimate and experiential knowledge of good and evil. This understanding is what would keep them entangled in the new state that they had entered.

It is interesting that the first thing they did after discovering they were now naked, was to hide from the presence of God amid the trees because of fear. The Bible says they "saw" that they were naked; something they hadn't noticed before. Somehow the new knowledge they had acquired caused them to look at themselves. The trees represented their environment, their home, and also the job and task they were given to do—to tend the garden. This is where we still hide today, in our environment, busy lives, and daily routines. There is a verse in Romans that describes this scenario quite well:

> I was once alive apart from the Law; but when the commandment came, sin became alive and I died; and this commandment, which was to result in life, proved to result in death for me; for sin, taking an opportunity through the commandment, **deceived** me and through it killed me. (Romans 7:9-11, emphasis mine)

This passage is an exact picture of what happened in the garden. In context, these verses are actually talking about a time in a child's life before he comes to the knowledge of good and evil. However, when Adam and Eve were first created, they were also in this same condition. They were alive, free, and had none of this knowledge. They were in a childlike state of innocence. The commandment that God gave them was never intended to bring death but instead it was meant to bring life. In fact it was meant to protect them; however, sin took an advantage through the commandment and brought death upon them. Notice how Eve said to God, "The serpent deceived me."

The Father's DNA

There is much speculation concerning why God chose to make mankind, and why He would put such a tree in the garden in the first place. It seems rather cruel to create something—a new species of being—and then set them up to fail. However, I believe a closer look at this idea can yield some amazing thoughts about the nature of our Father in heaven. In Genesis 1:26 it states that God was intending to make a creature in His "image" and in His "likeness." He had made all kinds of beings before, but this one was different even from the angels. He intended to make it like a "mini-Him." In keeping with that thought, if you were going to make a replica of yourself, would it be a true replica if you made it accurate down to the last detail, except for one defining point of your character? There is an interesting scripture verse that emphasizes this point in human terms:

> *When Adam had lived one hundred and thirty years, he became the father of a son in his own likeness, according to his image, and named him Seth.* (Genesis 5:3)

You see, God wanted children, and children are like their father and mother in every way; they have the same DNA. In order to make mankind in *His* image and likeness, He had to give them all of the basic parts that He had, including one thing He knew would be a chronic weakness for their existence on this planet. In fact, He didn't even give it to them right away, but He did make it available on a tree. It was the knowledge of good and evil. This knowledge was an essential attribute that God was all too familiar with. Before they ate, He tried to tell them of the responsibility of having a free will, and the consequence of eating, but they, no doubt, had little frame of reference for such words as "death" and

> God wanted children, and children are like their father and mother in every way; they have the same DNA.

"disobedience." After they ate, God stated that they had now become "like Him," knowing good from evil. Once again, likeness requires similarity to something.

Risk Beyond Comprehension

What is awe-inspiring to me about this thought is how much of a risk-taker God is. This is risk on a scale that cannot be measured in human terms and it is not the only area of creation in which God took risks. A couple of obvious examples come to mind immediately: money and human sexuality. The love of money is, as the Bible states, the root of all evil (1 Timothy 6:10). There has been untold greed, wars, bloodshed, and human power struggles all with money at the center of them. There is also such a beautiful side to the use of money. It can be used in a positive way for provision, care, and showing love. I am not sure what the ratio might be, but it seems infinitely more harm has been done with money in our world than good. However, to God, the risk of a small amount of beauty was worth creating this gift and giving it to us.

Human sexuality is much the same. The amount of devastation perpetrated through this gift is staggering. Think of the sex trades, prostitution, rape, incest, millions of babies being aborted, control issues, unwanted children, lust, homosexuality, hurt, etc.—not to mention the fact that the Bible tells us this gift is to be used within the context of marriage. In fact, in the Old Testament, sex defined marriage. However, in our world, I would venture to say that only a small percentage of the use of this gift would be considered holy according to a biblical model. Yet, to God, somehow the small chance of this gift being used in its beautiful and correct context was worth the risk of the countless heartaches it has caused over the history of human existence.

We will never know the infinite thought processes that went into God's decision to fashion us the way He did, taking a risk in making us unlike any other being ever created. He, without doubt, knew what the consequence would be, both for us and for Him. Somehow the potential for beauty to be experienced in a relationship with creations of His own kind was worth it. These motivations and measurements are His alone to sort out. As for me, I am completely undone by the magnitude of this love. Without hesitation or regret He created us in His image, and what a ride it has been ever since.

> *Without hesitation or regret God created us in His image, and what a ride it has been ever since.*

In the next pages we are going to take a closer look at the fruit of the tree of knowledge of good and evil and how it forever affected our world.

Chapter 3
The Blood and the Law

After the account in the first three chapters of Genesis, the tree of life disappears from the Bible altogether except, as mentioned, for a few isolated places in Proverbs, and Revelation. In Proverbs, it is mentioned figuratively rather than literally. It reappears literally in Revelation, the last book of the Bible. What ensues in the historical, biblical text is an overwhelmingly sad commentary on the state of the earth and of man. What is alarming is that mankind, now armed with the knowledge of

> *God is never without a plan, and we see Him begin to implement His plan for redemption (to buy back something which was lost).*

both good and evil, seems to habitually choose evil rather than good. God, however, is never without a plan, and we see Him begin to implement His plan for redemption (to buy back something which was lost) at the very beginning.

He began the buy-back process by making some declarations and we see this in Genesis 3:14-20. In particular, God speaks of the seed of the woman crushing the head of the serpent. This plan, however, was a long-term strategy that took almost 4000 years to put into action, and it was implemented in stages.

The First Sacrifice

The first stage was the shedding of blood to cover sin, which we see after the fall in Genesis: "The Lord God made garments of skin for Adam and his wife, and clothed them." (Genesis 3:21) We are not told exactly what happened here, but evidently some kind of sacrifice was made, animals were killed, blood was spilled, and God showed Adam and Eve that blood was needed to atone for the newfound, sinful condition they had chosen. This sacrifice, in turn, gave them temporary relief from having to look at their own fallen, naked condition. This point is further emphasized in the very next chapter of Genesis, when Cain and Abel brought their offerings before the Lord. Abel brought a choice animal from his flock, blood was spilled, and his offering was accepted. Cain, on the other hand, brought substandard fruit, and this offering was not accepted. Then, in Genesis 8, Noah offered a blood offering to the Lord after the flood. A bit later in Genesis, we see Abraham making the same kinds of offerings, as well as the famous account of Abraham and Isaac. We can surmise from these accounts that there was some sort of primitive, yet regular sacrificial system sanctioned and implemented by God.

But with this plan, things went from bad to worse. Things got so twisted on the earth that Genesis 6:5 states, "every intent of the thoughts of man's heart was evil continually." In other words, the knowledge (those things contained in mankind's mind) of good and evil had for the most part completely forsaken any good and gravitated to continual evil. The situation eventually degraded to the place where God could find only one righteous man on the earth—Noah—and He saved him and his family. The rest of the earth was destroyed with a flood and God started populating the earth again.

There is an interesting portion of Scripture in Romans that sheds some light on the condition that man was in during this stage of history:

> *Therefore, just as through one man sin entered into the world, and death through sin, and so death spread to all men, because all sinned—for until the Law, sin was in the world, but sin is not imputed when there is no law.*

Nevertheless death reigned from Adam until Moses, even over those who had not sinned, in the likeness of the offense of Adam, who is a type of Him who was to come. (Romans 5:12-14)

Let us navigate through a portion of this maze. These verses state that sin entered the world through one man, namely Adam, and death spread to all. However, it also states that unless there is a law that can be broken, there really can be no sin (here it is talking about the Mosaic Law). We know that the Mosaic Law came many years later, but there was still sin in the likeness of the offense of Adam. In other words, from Adam until Moses, people sinned in a manner resembling the way Adam sinned. This was mostly a transgression of disobedience and rebellion for they disobeyed God in eating the forbidden fruit. Then when Moses came along and wrote the Law, people sinned because they now had a standard to uphold (the Law) which they could not live up to. There are two slightly different reasons, or, if you like, "kinds of sin," both producing the same result: death.

The Mosaic Law

This brings us to the second stage of the redemptive plan of God. We see in the books of Exodus through Deuteronomy, the integration of the Law. This was done for the most part through Moses, and it was written down and put into practice during a time when the children of Israel (God's chosen people) were wandering in the desert on a forty-year journey to their promised land. This was a much more intricate and exacting system of sacrifices, feasts, laws, blessings, and curses. It was extremely comprehensive, and its text covers almost four books of the Bible. We are told quite clearly in Galatians 3 what the purpose of the Law was:

> *Why the Law then? It was added because of transgressions, having been ordained through the angels by the agency of a mediator, until the seed would come to whom the promise had been made. But before faith came, we were kept in custody under the Law, being shut up to the faith which was later to be revealed. Therefore the Law has become our tutor to lead us to Christ, so that we might be justified by faith.* (Galatians 3:19, 23- 24)

Here we see that the Law was added because of transgression, namely Adam's transgression. Things were such a mess that something had to be done for our own protection. And so, the Law was given to keep us in protective custody until the next stage of redemption, "faith in Jesus," could be revealed. It was also instated to show us how in our own strength, we are utterly incapable of keeping law. Another way of saying this is that the Law was put in place as a teaching tool to show us our weakness as humans. It points out that without Christ and grace we are absolutely lost and trapped in our fallen nature.

> *It is striking that the entire Law is based on one thing – the knowledge of good and evil.*

But what is even more interesting is the emphasis of this phase of redemption. It is striking that the entire Law is based on one thing – the knowledge of good and evil. There are positive laws ("Thou shalt ...") and there are negative laws ("Thou shalt not ... "). You shall do the good things and you shall not do the evil things. The first man and woman God placed on the earth had opted for the knowledge of good and evil as their living environment, so God had to come up with a system of redemption that would work in this context. In other words, if you can't beat it, join it. It is almost as if God was saying, "So you wanted the knowledge of good and evil. Alright, you have it. Now we are going to have to come up with a way that you can actually live and be successful under the system you have chosen. Here is a system of laws, rules, regulations, and statutes. If you follow them carefully you will live in My original blessing and prosper. If not, you will fall under the curse and die."

You might say that the Mosaic Law is the ultimate collection of the ordinances of good and evil. Almost every doable evil is mentioned here, as well as the correct way to live—the good. We are told not to worship idols and also how to worship God. We are told not to lie and, on the other hand, how to honor our parents. The children of Israel were given an honest chance here to follow after good. They were even told to isolate from the rest of the world (the evil portion) so that they would have a better chance at succeeding. They were not allowed to intermarry with other people groups, and when they went to battle with their enemies, they were told to destroy everything. They were also instructed not to make any covenants or agreements with the evil nations. Good and evil was written into their moral code and assimilated deep into their culture. It was lived out in the daily, weekly, monthly, and yearly cycles of their lives, and punctuated by periodic feasts, which were observed with strict consequence of failure. Once again, the blood sacrifice was at the center of this system to cover any shortfalls as far as sin went. This was indeed an elaborate and powerful model that was given. When it was all over, near the end of Deuteronomy, God literally begged them to choose life. If anybody could have managed to live successfully in an environment governed by the knowledge of good and evil, these people should have been able to do it.

We need, however, only read through a few more pages of biblical history to see the results of the new Law. Once again, these chosen and isolated people were incapable of following God's laws even for a few short generations. The rest of the Old Testament is a story of ups and downs as far as following the Law was concerned. They would take a step forward when a godly leader would arise and then fall two steps back when that leadership would change hands. Eventually this cycle turned into taking a step forward and numerous steps back until they were so far from God that they were taken into captivity. Even this amazing Law that they were given was not enough to give them the power for a successful life. In fact, it was failing miserably.

Once again, the knowledge of good and evil was edging dangerously towards the evil side. God would bring them back and set them up again, but they would fail shortly thereafter. This pattern repeated until the history books were so darkened that there is a period of nearly four hundred years that is not even recorded. We know that during this era Israel was, for the most part, in captivity. Eventually when they reappear in the New Testament, they are under Roman rule, detainees in their own land. We also know that they had taken the Law to a whole new level by adding hundreds of sub-laws to the account written in the Bible. Here they had become intimidated by their own Law, and to avoid breaking it, they wrote more human laws in order to keep them from breaking the core Spirit inspired laws. This became a heavy, religious system of rules and regulations that was nearly impossible to follow, and devoid of compassion. It also became the catalyst for the events leading up to our Savior's eventual crucifixion.

Hopelessly Obsessed with Good and Evil

At this time, let us step back and take a brief look at religion in general. At the center of any religion is a set of rules and regulations that govern the activities of its followers. As humans, it is built into our very nature that we follow rules of good and evil. We can, in fact, live no other way. We inevitably write rules that tell us about the good we should do, and also what is bad and how to avoid it. Then the ones who follow the rules get the kudos, or the Zen, or make it to a paradise like afterlife, and the evil ones supposedly go to the bad place, hell, or come back as a mosquito rather than a

> *As humans, it is built into our very nature that we follow rules of good and evil. We can, in fact, live no other way.*

higher form of life. This is our pathetic attempt to live up to the system of knowledge that we chose right from the start. It doesn't matter the religion, the knowledge of good and evil is always right in the middle.

It is also interesting how we as humans are obsessed with good and evil outside the context of religion. One of the first protests a non-Christian person will levy at someone telling him/her that he/she needs to receive Christ in order to inherit eternal life is: "But, I am a good person!" The truth is that being good has never had anything to do with it. We only think it does because of our preoccupation with the subject of good and evil, and so we hold this as the highest standard a person can reach for: to be a good person. In reality, our spiritual inheritance has always had everything to do with a relationship with our God and Father, and any good that happens is an effortless overflow of that relationship. However, we as humans forsook that relationship way back in the garden. Now we try to appease our consciences, or make it to a successful afterlife by being good. Even Santa Claus knows that if you are good you get a better gift, and if you are naughty you get a lump of coal; and all of this doing good is done completely on our own strength. There is a verse in Matthew that speaks clearly of this scenario:

> *Many will say to Me on that day, "Lord, Lord, did we not prophesy in Your name, and in Your name cast our demons, and in Your name perform many miracles?" And then I will declare to them, "I never knew you; depart from Me, you who practice lawlessness." (Matthew 7:22)*

This passage is telling and sobering indeed. Here it states that there are people going around doing good things; some of them are even happening in the name of the Lord Jesus Himself. However, the response in the end is that the Master never knew them. I heard someone give an illustration of this scenario one time that made a lot of sense to me.

Imagine for a moment what it would be like if you came to the end of your life and went to the biggest, most beautiful house in the world and knocked on the door. The owner would then come to the door and ask you what you want. You would in turn say, "I would like to come into your house and live with you." The owner would look at you and ask why you should be let in to which you would reply, "I should be let in because I am a good person." The owner of the house would, of course, not let you in because he has no clue as to the identity of the person standing in front of him. You, in other words, have absolutely no relationship with him—he doesn't know you. On the other hand, if you knew the house owner, were a relative of his, or especially if you were a son or daughter of his, he would likely let you in even if you had done a few bad things.

Notice the last phrase of this Scripture verse: "depart from Me, you who practice lawlessness." The Bible tells us that if we break even one small, miniscule law, we are guilty of breaking the whole Law. We can try to be as good as possible, but in the end we are going to be guilty of breaking the Law however we look at it. Consequently, we are put in a position of lawlessness; a direct result of the knowledge of good and evil.

Sin and the Law

At this point in time it might be helpful to examine a couple of verses in the New Testament which describe the condition that we have ended up in quite remarkably. First, let us look at Romans 7 in the specific context of someone under the system of the Law. The Apostle Paul was talking about his old life under the Mosaic Law as a Pharisee, and how zealous he was of keeping and defending this Law. This passage is the follow-up to his narrative:

> *What shall we say then? Is the Law sin? May it never be! On the contrary, I would not have come to know sin except through the Law; for I would not have known about coveting if the Law had not said, "You shall not covet." But sin, taking opportunity through the commandment, produced in me coveting of every kind; for apart from the Law, sin is dead.* (Romans 7:7-8)

This is an amazing portion of Scripture. It says that the Law is actually good; however, it tells us about certain evils. The reason it tells us about them is in hope that we won't do these things. But then, merely because we know about the evil, sin takes its opportunity and we end up doing the very thing that we are not supposed to do. It also says that if we didn't have this knowledge (in this example, knowledge about coveting) we wouldn't be tempted to covet because we wouldn't even know that this particular sin exists: "apart from the Law, sin is dead." It has no life. Here is one more interesting Scripture verse, "The sting of death is sin, and the power of sin is the Law." (1 Corinthians 15:56)

Here it states that death is caused by sin, but the power of sin is the Law. This verse reveals something about human nature that is most disturbing and most beautiful in the same breath. Once we see or know something, we have little resistance to it. In order for God to create us in His image, this part of our nature was a necessity. The fact is we have been made free, so free that we most often have no idea what to do with our freedom. So how did we handle this amazing gift? We rejected it and exchanged our freedom for knowledge of good and evil, and subsequently law. This is why we, as humans, are much more comfortable with the idea of rules, regulations, and religion than with the freedom of relationship and blessing which we were originally offered. It also gives us an amazing window into the personality of our Father God. He is not a micromanager or a control freak. Instead, He is all about releasing those He loves into incomprehensible liberty. When He created us, He was serious about letting us do what we desired. Even faced with a bad decision, He would rather let us live with the consequences than violate our freedom. Once again, what a stunning risk God took in making us the way He did! It was one that without question He knew would eventually cost Him everything.

Let's remember again the account of Eve in the garden. The first thing that she did was look at the forbidden tree. Once she did this, the temptation was already as good as over. When a thought is put into our minds, our nature is to follow through on this thought. This can be tragic in the negative sense, but beautiful in the positive sense. However, with a fallen sin-nature, once we have knowledge of an evil and we look at it, we more often than not tend to do that very thing. In this case our sin-nature rises up and drives us to the thing that we do not necessarily even want to do. This paradox is further illustrated in subsequent verses in Romans 7. Here Paul continues, once

> *Our Father God is not a micromanager or a control freak. Instead, He is all about releasing those He loves into incomprehensible liberty.*

again, this time in the "first person," from the viewpoint of someone under the Mosaic Law system:

> *For we know that the Law is spiritual, but I am flesh, sold into bondage to sin. For what I am doing, I do not understand; for I am not practicing what I would like to do, but I am doing the very thing I hate. But if I do the very thing I do not want to do, I agree with the Law, that the Law is good. So now, no longer am I the one doing it, but the sin which dwells in me. For I know that nothing good dwells in me, that is in my flesh; for the willing is present in me, but the doing of good is not. For the good that I want, I do not do, but I practice the very evil that I do not want.* (Romans 7:14–19)

Notice how the words "good" and "evil" are used in this text. Let's take a look at exactly how this system works to defeat us. When Adam and Eve ate the fruit of this tree, their link to God was severed. They were left in a condition of sin. Sin in the Bible can be found in two different contexts. The first is an act that you do which is wrong, such as the act of eating of the forbidden fruit. The second is the subsequent condition we find ourselves in when separated from God. In this state, our very nature has taken on the condition of sin and become fallen; thus we are said to have a "sin-nature." Here, we have no connection or relationship with God, and our spirit is dead rather than alive. We are, essentially, orphaned from our heavenly Father. Also, in this position, there is no way that the Holy Spirit of God can live in us because He cannot live in an unholy environment.

The Sin-nature

This condition of inheriting a "sin-nature" is the way every person since Adam and Eve has been born. It is passed on to every person born on the planet Earth through the seed of the father at the moment of conception (Psalm 51:5). So, we all enter this world with a sin-nature. We are also all bound to live by the knowledge of good and evil, which was poured out at the point of the eating of the fruit in the garden. For this reason, as the passage of Scripture we just read states, when we see or have knowledge of evil things, our sin-nature kicks in and drives us towards the evil. It doesn't matter much if we know about the good. We might even want to do the good, but our nature drives us towards the evil. Once a thought is put in our mind, we are already half way there, as the saying goes. So, Satan tempts us with evil, and puts things in front of us, or we see them ourselves, and away we go.

This tendency is our greatest weakness as a species. It has led us to the brink of extinction once already as recorded in the Bible, and if we read through to the end of Revelation, it will do so again before this world comes to an end. It is indeed a fallen condition that we are born into without Christ. A life separated from God, with an inborn sin-nature and a working knowledge of good and evil makes us highly susceptible to following after evil. Paul states in the same chapter of Romans, in a passage already quoted and discussed, that there is a short time in a person's life when he or she is innocent. This is a period in our childhood when we have no knowledge of good or evil. There is no "commandment," as the Bible calls it. However, as soon as this commandment comes to a child at what we call the age of accountability, they become spiritually dead. The knowledge of good and evil is a killer indeed. As you can see, there is good reason why God did not want us to eat from this tree.

A life separated from God, with an inborn sin-nature and a working knowledge of good and evil makes us highly susceptible to following after evil.

With this setting in mind, we will now turn the pages of our Bible over to the New Testament, in which we will find the Birth of God's Son, the Savior of the world. We will see the reason God needed to send Jesus to the earth without an earthly father. He had to supply the seed to a virgin through the Holy Spirit instead of a man so the sin-nature wouldn't be passed on to the Savior. We were destitute, in dire need of someone to free us from the condition that we chose back in the garden. We will explore this subject in greater depth in the following chapter.

Chapter 4
The Savior

What Jesus did on the earth was remarkable. He was given the same basic starting point as Adam and Eve: an earthly body, soul, and spirit without a sin-nature. He was born into full fellowship with God, having no separation from Him in spirit, soul, or body. This is the same status the first Adam enjoyed and for that reason Paul refers to Jesus as the "second Adam" (1 Corinthians 15:45). However, there was one part of His existence that wasn't the same. The first Adam had no knowledge of good and evil to contend with, and even so he fell fast and hard. The second Adam was born into a world fully ruled by the condition of the knowledge of good and evil. There is a noteworthy reference in the Old Testament that supports this thought:

> *Behold, a virgin will be with child and bear a son, and she will call His name Immanuel. He will eat curds and honey*

at the time He knows enough to refuse evil and choose good. (Isaiah 7:14-15)

This often quoted Christmas scripture speaks of the birth of Jesus. It then tells of a time in His life when He is eating curds and honey—the food of a young child. It goes on to explain that at this tender age, He would gain the necessary knowledge to "refuse evil and choose good." These verses describe quite remarkably, the progression in Jesus' life through the age of accountability. After this transition, it would be necessary for Him to live the rest of His life in the context of good and evil, never once slipping up, in order to succeed. Here is a passage that explains Jesus' assignment:

But when the fullness of time came, God sent forth His Son, born of a woman, born under the Law, so that He might redeem those who were under the Law, that we might receive the adoption as sons. (Galatians 4:4-5)

Jesus states very early in His public ministry that He came to fulfill the Law to the last dotted "i" and crossed "t" (Matthew 5:17-18). The Mosaic Law is the ultimate document containing the chronicles of good and evil, and remember; Jesus was born under this Mosaic system when it was at its most religious phase. As was mentioned earlier, the Jewish leaders had added hundreds of other laws to the ancient text making it an obstacle course that was nearly impossible to navigate. But if that wasn't enough, there is one more amazing thing that Jesus did:

> *Have this attitude in yourselves which was in Christ Jesus, who although He existed in the form of God, did not regard equality with God a thing to be grasped, but emptied Himself, taking on the form of a bond-servant, being made in the likeness of men. Being found in appearance as a man, He humbled Himself by becoming obedient to the point of death, even death on a cross.* (Philippians 2:5-8)

Here it clearly states that if Jesus could have had any advantage to succeed in His mission of redemption by being the Son of God, He emptied Himself, or gave up this privilege, and became just like us, in the likeness of men. This reminds me of the story in the Old Testament about Elijah on Mount Carmel, facing off against the prophets of Baal. He had them throw water on

> *Jesus stripped Himself of any advantage He might have had as God's Son and became like us.*

the sacrifice three times so that if fire came down from heaven, there would be no doubt of its origins (1 Kings 18:20-46). Likewise, Jesus stripped Himself of any advantage He might have had as God's Son and became like us. This way, when He would defeat the enemy, there would be no doubt about the legitimacy of His victory. This is why in the context of His earthly life, ministry, and the cross He was always called the "son of man."

This was His makeup. He was a man living in a normal body. He did not have a sin-nature, but He was privy to the knowledge of good and evil and all of its pitfalls. His temptations were very real and enticing. He had a connection to God because He had never sinned, so the Spirit of God lived inside of Him. Then, when He came out of the river at baptism, the Holy Spirit descended upon Him and remained on Him. Basically, He was in the same condition as any now born again man or woman. He was sin free, in fellowship with God, baptized in water, and "filled with" or "baptized in" the Holy Spirit inside and out.

If He had taken any other advantage, there is no possible way He could have been our Redeemer. He would have had tools with which to destroy the works of the enemy that subsequently, we would not have access to. He also could never have made a statement such as: "greater works than I shall you do because I go to My Father." (John 14:12) You have to remember that Satan is an extreme legalist, and Jesus' victory would have been forever contested by the Devil.

The Golden Rule

So how did Jesus navigate the obstacles of the knowledge of good and evil, or the "cannon of the Law?" There are several places where we find keys to His success. The first one is in the book of Matthew:

In everything, therefore, treat people the same way you want them to treat you, for this is the Law and the Prophets. (Matthew 7:12)

Here Jesus claims that the entire Law and Prophets can be summed up in one simple statement: treat others as you would want them to treat you. This maxim is sometimes called the "golden rule," a saying most of us have heard at least a few times in our

> *Jesus was able to boil the essence of numerous books of the Bible down to one rule rather than hundreds of pages of do's and don'ts.*

lives. It is incredible that Jesus was able to boil the essence of numerous books of the Bible down to one rule rather than hundreds of pages of do's and don'ts. The Law was exceedingly complex, but Jesus' new saying was profoundly simple. Notice also that it was a "good" or positive rule, not a "stay away from evil" or negative rule. There is a similar statement later in Matthew:

> *And He said to him, 'you shall love the Lord your God with all your heart, and with all your soul, and with all your mind.' This is the great and foremost commandment. The second is like it, 'you shall love your neighbor as yourself.' On these two commandments depend the whole Law and Prophets.* (Matthew 22:37-40)

Here Jesus adds one additional nuance to His golden rule: the part about loving God with all your heart, soul, and mind. Then He basically gives us a variation of the golden rule: love your neighbor as yourself, or in other words, treat others like you would want them to treat you. Keep in mind however, that a law, even if it is a good law, is still a law.

In John we see similar verses but here Jesus raises the bar to a whole new level. In fact, the bar of loving one another is set so high there is no earthly way we can do what Jesus commands on our own:

> *Just as the Father has loved me, I have also loved you; abide in my love. This is my commandment, that you love one another, just as I have loved you.* (John 15:9, 12)

Here we are given a new commandment that is impossible for a human being to keep. God the Father is actually made out of two things according to the Bible: light and love (1 John 1:5; 4:16). If He were somehow to be wounded, instead of blood oozing from the wound, light and love would come out. In this text, we are no longer asked to love our neighbor as we love our self: we are told to love our neighbor as Jesus loved us. However, we are also reminded that Jesus loves us the same way the Father loves Him (remember, the Father is the One who is actually made out of love). My friends, if we are going to love as Jesus loved us, and by extrapolation as the Father loved Him, we are going to need some serious help. This love is so far beyond what we can comprehend it tests the outer limits of our finite minds. There is, however, help for this task, and in due course we will discuss the source of this help.

> God the Father is actually made out of two things according to the Bible: light and love.

The life of Jesus as recorded in the gospels was extremely comprehensive and we could spend a lifetime searching for clues to how He managed to live a sinless life. In my estimation, here are a few other keys that contributed to Jesus' success of fulfilling the Mosaic Law; the canonized embodiment of the knowledge of good and evil.

Religion and Relationship Separated

Jesus was very hard on religion and deliberately broke many religious regulations. Here is a partial list of things He did that didn't go over very well with His contemporaries, the synagogue leaders: He broke rules of fasting, washing, and eating; He was called a glutton and a wine bibber; He rubbed out heads of grain on the Sabbath for a snack with His disciples; He healed on the Sabbath; He hung out with undesirable people; He talked to women when alone with them; He associated with prostitutes; He allowed a former prostitute to pour perfume all over Him and wash His feet with her hair and tears; He set a woman caught in adultery free; He threw people out of the temple with a whip for buying and selling in the lobby of a church (I don't even want to know what would happen if we had that rule today); and He went to dinner at a tax collector's house.

Jesus knew these things were not important to God, and He went through life not caring about points of contention that didn't matter. He knew that living a life free from sin was not about keeping trivial, religious rules, but that it was about the relationship He had with His Father in heaven. He talked about Him often and spoke of the mutual love they shared.

The Ultimate Prayer Enthusiast

We find Jesus many times disappearing or slipping away to the wilderness to pray. Here are some examples:

After He had sent the crowds away, He went up on the mountain by Himself to pray; and when it was evening, He was there alone. (Matthew 14:23)

In the early morning, while it was still dark, Jesus got up, left the house, and went away to a secluded place, and was praying there. (Mark 1:35)

> *To Jesus, prayer was more than a religious exercise; it was an encounter with the Father and the very atmosphere of heaven.*

Here are a few additional scriptures you can look up on your own, all saying the same basic thing: Mark 6:46; Luke 5:16; 6:12; and John 6:15. Now here is one more verse:

Some eight days after these sayings, He took along Peter and John and James, and went up on the mountain to pray. (Luke 9:28)

I mention this passage for a specific reason. It is Luke's account of the Mount of Transfiguration. Up until this time nobody had seen Jesus on one of His all-night prayer vigils, but here He allowed three of His disciples a unique window into His prayer life. You see, to Jesus, prayer was more than a religious exercise; it was an encounter with the Father and the very atmosphere of heaven. There is absolutely no way a person could pray for days and nights on end the way most of us pray. What Jesus was doing was accessing realms of glory in His prayer life. On this mountain He became glorified and left a high water mark for us in our prayer life. Here is another scripture that explains this a little further: "And no one hath ascended into heaven, but he that descended out of heaven, even the Son of man, who is in heaven." (John 3:13)

Once again, Jesus was ascending and descending into spiritual places while He was praying. Whether this was actually in body or only in spirit, He was experiencing the glory of this domain. We have been invited into this same experience.

An Unshakeable Identity

Immediately following Jesus' water baptism, a dove descended upon Him and a voice from heaven declared, "This is my beloved Son in whom I am well pleased." Directly after this event, Jesus was led out into the wilderness to be tempted. Each ensuing temptation started with Satan calling into question the heavenly identity Jesus had just received by taunting, "If you are the Son of God, do this ..." Jesus never once flinched—He stood firm in who He was and in the word He had been given.

Solid in the Word

Jesus rebuffed every temptation of the enemy with, "It is written." Keep in mind that the scriptures He quoted were directly the Mosaic Law. Jesus was serious about finishing His assignment by fulfilling every letter of the Law. In the end, He would beat the system of the knowledge of good and evil hands down—fairly and squarely.

By the end of Jesus' life, both the rulers of the day and Satan tired of trying to catch Him in a religious contradiction. Every time they attempted it, He would answer with such grace and simplicity that they found themselves wishing they had never challenged Him in the first place. Eventually we read this verse: "Some of the scribes answered and said, 'Teacher, You have spoken well.' For they did not have the courage to question Him any longer about anything." (Luke 20:39-40) After this, they decided it was best to just try and put Him to death. We know this was a demonically inspired idea because of the following scripture: "The wisdom which none of the rulers of this age has understood; for if they had understood it they would not have crucified the Lord of Glory." (1 Corinthians 2:8) This was religion, law, and evil at its lowest point in history. It was so low, in fact, it decided to kill its own Savior. In the next chapter we will examine some of the realities of the cross and how it forever affected life on planet Earth.

Chapter 5
The Grace Tree

It has been said that the cross changed everything. This is more than true. What Jesus accomplished on the cross was, without doubt, the greatest and most courageous act since the beginning of creation. We can read about it in all four Gospels, each account giving us a slightly different perspective on this deed of love.

In this chapter it is not my goal to give a description of the cross, as there are many volumes published on this wonder. Instead, I would like

> *There was a very deliberate line drawn in the sand at the cross; the dividing line between law and grace.*

to view it from a bit of a different angle—one that carries through with our theme.

There was a very deliberate line drawn in the sand at the cross; the dividing line between law and grace. Before the cross we see a world ruled by law, and in the chapters up to now, our discussions have centered on the Law, its origins, and its mode of operation. In contrast, after the cross we see a world released into grace. This sacrifice is the cleaving point of history: it leaves nothing undone; forever realigning the way man relates to his God. Subsequently, from here on our discussions will gravitate towards the wonder of grace. Remember the reason for the cross: it was to redeem those held in bondage under the Law. Thus Jesus had to die at the hand of the Law.

One with Christ

These things being said, there is an ageless wonder I would like to draw out in this section: when Jesus went to the cross, we actually became "one" with Him. An understanding of this idea is essential for us to proceed with our discussion on the subject of grace. We will illustrate this concept with two separate thoughts that at first might seem unrelated, but at the end both point to the same thing. Please bear with me as we attempt to explain a very theological concept in simple terms.

Let us first go to the book of John. We will look at a selection of verses in what is called the "High Priestly Prayer." It is the prayer Jesus prayed the night He went to the cross. Here, while praying for His disciples, Jesus says some beautiful and strange things:

> *I am no longer in the world; and yet they themselves are in the world, and I come to You. Holy Father, keep them in Your name, the name that You have given Me, that they may be one even as We are one.* (John 17:11)

A few verses later, Jesus prays the same thing but this time for all who would follow down through the ages:

> *I do not ask on behalf of these alone, but for those also who believe in Me through their word; that they may all be one; even as You, Father are in me and I in You; that they also may be in Us, so that the world might believe that You sent me.* (John 17:19-20)

A little while later Jesus prays one more time:

> *The glory which You have given Me I have given to them, that they may be one, just as We are one; I in them and You in Me, that they may be perfected in unity, so that the world may know that You sent Me.* (John 17:22-23)

Now, let us take a closer look at these scriptures. I have heard many people talk, write, and sing about this idea. Most of the discussion focuses on the perception that when Jesus prayed for His disciples to be made one, He was asking that there not be any divisions among them. However, if one thing is clear from history, it is the fact that divisions have run rampant in the body of Christ. There are hundreds of sects and denominations worldwide, some even causing bloodshed and war. If we look at this scenario it would seem the Father didn't answer Jesus' prayer. Even though the thought of perfect harmony among believers is most appealing, I do not believe this is what He meant. Instead, there is a verse in Galatians that sheds some light on this mystery for us:

> *There is neither Jew nor Greek, there is neither slave nor free man, there is neither male nor female; for you are all **one** in Christ Jesus.* (Galatians 3:28, emphasis mine)

This passage indicates that the Father did answer Jesus' prayer by making us all "one" in Christ. Now let's go back to the night before the crucifixion and explore this idea. Jesus asks the Father for something incomprehensible: that we could be all made "one." Then He explains, "Even as You, Father, are in me and I in You; that they also may be in Us."

This is the part about the cross I find most stunning: when Jesus prayed this prayer, He was petitioning the Father for each and every individual that would ever exist—past, present, and future—to be made as if they were the only "one" ever created. Because God is no respecter of persons

(Acts 10:34), there is absolutely no distinction of age, race, gender, or social status. This thought takes my breath away every time I ponder it.

With Him on the Cross

Have you ever heard the statement, "If you were the only person on the earth, Jesus would have still gone to the cross for you?" Well, in the eyes of Jesus that day, there was only one person He was dying for: you. This is one of the great mysteries of the cross: redemption for mankind as a whole, yet a personal and intimate redemption for each individual. Then He clarified, *"them in Us."*

Here, Jesus asked for the Father to place each and every person in His heart—"in Him," if you like. In other words, Jesus was asking for us to be made "one" in being with Him. Then He did something unthinkable: He went to the cross and literally carried each and every one of us in His heart through the entire experience. Sometimes in liturgy this is referred to as the "mystical union," Jesus and His Bride, united on the cross.

This reality is what makes the cross so amazing: you and I were with Him on that cross; in fact we were "in Him." We were made one, united with Him, and everything He went through, we went through, except we didn't know it was happening. It should have been our cross, but instead He carried each one of us in His heart while taking the cross on our behalf.

> You and I were with Him on that cross; in fact we were "in Him."

I want you to imagine this scenario for a moment. Think of the cross and what Jesus went through. Picture each wound, every blow, the nails, and the scorn. Don't view it from the outside position of yourself looking at the cross while Jesus suffers. Instead, see it from the perspective of Jesus carrying you inside His heart as He suffers on your behalf. This is truly a wonder of all wonders.

Here we find the beginning of a profound concept in the New Testament: being "in Christ." It is mentioned numerous times with great and beautiful promises attached to it. This identification started right there, that day on the cross. Let us also remember Jesus did this all for us "while we were yet sinners" (Romans 5:8), and He did it for every single person born—past, present, and future—on the planet Earth. All we have to do is receive this gift. Talk about a love far and beyond all other loves!

The Baptism of the Cross

Here is a second thought in relation to the cross and our union with Christ, concerning baptism, in a statement made by Jesus a few weeks prior to His crucifixion: "But I have a baptism to undergo, and how distressed I am until it is accomplished." (Luke 12:50) Jesus is plainly talking about His impending death, and He is referring to it as a baptism. There is another similar group of verses in Mark, in which two of Jesus' disciples came to Him and asked for a special request. They wanted to know if He would grant them to sit on His right and left in the new kingdom of glory. This was His reply:

> But Jesus said to them, "you do not know what you are asking. Are you able to drink the cup that I drink, or to be baptized with the baptism with which I am baptized?" They said to Him, "we are able." And Jesus said to them, "The cup that I drink you shall drink; and you shall be baptized with the baptism with which I am baptized." (Mark 10:38-39)

These verses also tell of Jesus' death, and again He refers to it as a baptism, and also a cup He must drink. Then He tells His disciples (we know them to be James and John) that they will someday be baptized in the same way and drink the same cup. Let us go for a moment with this visual and see where it takes us. First, Jesus was crucified. In this experience, He took on the very nature that we had opted for in the first place—the sin-nature.

> *And He Himself bore our sins in His body on the cross, so that we might die to sin and live to righteousness; for by His wounds you were healed.* (1 Peter 2:24)

Notice this scripture states: He bore our sins in His body. This action was necessary because the sin-nature resides in our bodies. Not only did He take on this nature, He took every act of sin, sickness, poverty, and hellish curse ever conceived of.

I realize there are various traditional ways of being baptized, but in the circles in which I grew up, it only meant one thing: being slam-dunked beneath the ice cold waters of the river that flowed past our church camp! If there is one thing I remember from this experience, it is the fact that I had to give up control to the person who was baptizing me. I had to trust that they were not going to drown me. Likewise, when Jesus said: "Father, into Your hands I commit My spirit," He was giving up His life as an act of faith, trusting His Father to bring Him up from the grave again (John 23:46). Then Jesus gave up His spirit, died, and went down into the earth. This is a visual parallel of going under the water in baptism.

We don't know exactly what happened next, but there are numerous places in the Bible that give us clues. If we connect these scriptural dots, we can conclude that Jesus was likely taken down to the region of hell, where He suffered even more. What we do know is that by the time three days and nights were completed, Jesus had paid the price for every single act of sin and the ensuing curse; past, present, and future. Jesus was then resurrected from the dead and came up out of that place victorious. He also brought the spirits of many righteous people with Him, and some of them even came out of the graves at that time. Once again, this is a visual image of rising up out of the waters of baptism into a new, resurrected life.

What we have just described is the baptism of the cross from Jesus' point of view. Now let's look at some verses which describe this same scenario from a different point of view; this one being ours.

> *Or do you not know that all of us who have been baptized into Christ Jesus have been baptized into His death? Therefore we have been buried with Him through baptism into death, so that as Christ was raised from the dead through the glory of the Father, so we too might walk in newness of life. For if we have become **united** with Him in the likeness of His death, certainly we shall also be in the*

likeness of His resurrection, knowing this, that our old self was crucified with Him, in order that our body of sin might be done away with. (Romans 6:3-7, emphasis mine)

Here we are told about the baptism of the cross and our united experience with Jesus. First, we were baptized into His death. As He died, we died with Him on that cross. This scripture actually says "our old self was crucified with Him," a profound statement in itself. Then we were buried with Him in that tomb. After that, when Jesus was raised from the dead, we became alive together with Him in His resurrection. Notice how it states that we have become "united" with Him in His death, burial, and resurrection. It now becomes evident what Jesus was talking about earlier when he said to His disciples, "you will also be baptized with the same baptism that I am." Once again, we were right there, "one" with Him, "in Him" as He went through the entire process. The word "united" is the word that is used in Church liturgy to describe our mystical union or "unio mystica" with Christ as consummated on the cross.

> *H*e has already accepted us. Now we need only whisper His name and the deal is done.

Because of this unification, one of the first things we are told to do after repenting of our sins and receiving Christ (the born-again experience), is to be baptized. It is a powerful visual representation of what Jesus went through on the cross and how we were united with Him in the entire experience. It is also a public declaration of our acceptance of that union with His death, burial, and resurrection. He has already accepted us. Now we need only whisper His name and the deal is done.

The Baptism of "One"

There is one more passage of Scripture that we will look at before leaving this idea. It is found in Galatians and we have already referenced it once in this chapter.

> *But now that faith has come, we are no longer under a tutor* [the Law is the tutor being referred to here]. *For you are all sons of God through faith in Jesus Christ. For all of you who were* **baptized into Christ Jesus** *have clothed yourselves with Christ. There is neither Jew nor Greek, there is neither slave nor free man, there is neither male nor female; for you are all* **one** *in Christ Jesus.* (Galatians 3:25-29, emphasis mine)

This selection of verses ties both the concept of "baptism" and being made "one" together in the same place. They are, in fact, one and the same. It also makes clear that we have now been set free from the Law.

Now that we have established how we became one with Jesus as He went to the cross, we will return to our theme of the knowledge of good and evil versus life, and discuss the cross in this context.

Let us return again to the beginning. If you will recall, there were two trees in the middle of the garden. We have spent a great deal of time discussing the realities that were released into the world through eating from the tree of "the knowledge of good and evil." It only makes sense that the ultimate goal of Jesus on the cross would be to restore us back to "garden conditions" once again. He literally came to restore us to the same condition that we fell from in the first place. Anything less would have been a failure.

In order to accomplish this, He would need to release some vital realities that were in the original garden that we, as humans, need to be successful and free. In my mind, there are two essentials here. First, He would need to restore us back to innocence, to a condition where we were no longer bound to live by the knowledge of good and evil—in other words, the Law. This status would need to include bringing us back to "pre-bite of the forbidden tree" territory. Second, once returned to this condition, He would need to give us access to the tree of life again. Its fruit would be necessary to restore the freedom, life, and regeneration of our bodies, souls, and spirits needed to live above the curse.

The Passover

There are a couple of Old Testament vignettes of this life-giving and innocent environment. The first is when the children of Israel were about to leave Egypt: the feast of Passover. If you look at the crucifixion experience of Jesus, it actually happened during the Jewish feast of Passover. The instructions of Moses were very specific, and are found in Exodus 12:1-13. In short, they were to take a lamb, kill it, put some of the blood on their doorposts and lintels, and then eat the lamb along with unleavened bread. This was all to be done with staff in hand, and sandals on their feet, ready to leave slavery for good. This feast is, of course, a foreshadowing of the cross. The doorposts and lintel were made of wood in those days, which represents the tree Jesus suffered on. The results from the Passover celebration were impressive. First, God's people were saved from death even though it was happening all around them. Second, when they left, they plundered Egypt, taking with them much wealth. Third, they were completely healed. Psalm 105 states that there was not one feeble person among them.

The Serpent on a Standard

The second vignette is in the story of the bronze serpent on the pole. This account is found in Numbers 21:6-9. The children of Israel had grumbled against God and found themselves among fiery serpents. The snakes were biting and killing many of them. Moses interceded to the Lord and was instructed to set up a bronze serpent on a tall standard. Anyone who looked at the pole and serpent would be healed from the snakes' venom. This picture, again, is a type of the cross. We, as a human race, were living in an environment where the serpent (Satan) was afflicting us in many different ways. In the end, Jesus was lifted up on a tree taking on sin, death, and the curse, and if we look to Him we will live.

What I want to point out in this second story is the usage of the tree to affix the bronze serpent to. As we know, Jesus was crucified on a tree, and this was necessary in order to redeem us from the curse:

> *Christ redeemed us from the curse of the Law, having become a curse for us—for it is written, 'Cursed is everyone who hangs on a tree.'* (Galatians 3:13)

The Tree of Life Rediscovered

To conclude this chapter I would like to propose something that, in my estimation, is one of the most profound and beautiful pictures in all of history. In the beginning, there was a magnificent, life-infused tree in the middle of the Garden of Eden. It was no doubt impregnated with the very glory of heaven. The presence and fragrance of God surrounded it, and it was there for everyone. All one had to do was look at this tree, then reach out, take, and eat. Remember, this was the sequence of events that started Eve on the downward spiral with the wrong tree. We have also discussed how this process would have been the same with the tree of life.

What I would like to suggest is that even though the tree of life disappears after Genesis 3, not to be seen again literally until the new heaven and earth, it actually does re-appear. In fact, it has been right under our noses ever since our Savior died on it almost two thousand years ago. The cross that Jesus suffered on is, without

> *The cross that Jesus suffered on is, without doubt, the re-incarnated tree of life.*

doubt, the re-incarnated tree of life. However, because of the mess we have made of our world, the knowledge of good and evil we have chosen, bloodshed, sin, and the curse, it looks quite different now.

It is no longer a big, colorful, stunning looking tree with green leaves that are for the healing of the nations, and tasty fruit that, when consumed, will make one live forever (Revelation 22:2). It is now a bloody, repulsive, and disturbing rough trunk of wood with an innocent man hanging on it. This is our Savior; unconditionally melded into the tree, beaten beyond recognition, and wearing a crown of thorns on His head. He is dying for our fallen condition, while tenderly carrying His lost Bride in His heart through the entire experience. This tree no longer has its roots spread into the ground of our world because it could not live in a cursed ground. Instead, it is stuck in a hole in the earth and yet still it reaches upward and outward, its branches now supporting nail-pierced hands. But, to those who love the cross, it is no less beautiful than that original tree in the garden. It also has no less life-giving, regenerative power, and no weaker infusion of the glory of heaven within it. It is the grace tree. Look upon it, take, and eat from it, and you will live forever in a condition of innocence.

Back to the Garden

There is one more detail to note: it was in the Garden of Gethsemane that Jesus made the final decision to surrender His will to the impending realities of the cross (Matthew 26:39-44, John 18:1). It was in a garden area in which He was crucified, and it was also in a garden tomb in which He was placed and then resurrected from (John 19:41). Jesus has indeed brought us back to the garden once again. In the next pages we will discuss the fruit of the tree of life, which is grace upon grace, and how it contrasts with the fruit of the tree of knowledge of good and evil.

Chapter 6
The Contrast

For of His fullness we have all received, and grace upon
grace. For the Law was given through Moses; grace and
truth were realized through Jesus Christ. (John 1:16-17)

There are many contrasts in the Bible, such as between
faith and fear. These two concepts are opposites, and are
often highlighted in a single verse, for example, "Why are
you so fearful? How is it that you have no faith?" (Mark 4:40
NKJV) Other contrasts are more obvious like love and hate,
life and death, or the curse and the blessing. However, there
is one contrast referred to over and over again in the New
Testament. This distinction can be a bit puzzling because at
first glance, these two things don't appear to have much to
do with each other in real life. The unlikely contrast I am
referring to is between law and grace. The verse that started
this chapter is only one of many Scripture verses that speak

of these two opposing concepts. Here is a partial list of a few others:

> *For sin shall not be master over you, for you are not under* **law** *but under* **grace**. (Romans 6:14, emphasis mine)

> *What then? Shall we sin because we are not under* **law** *but under* **grace**? *May it never be!* (Romans 6:15, emphasis mine)

> *I do not nullify the* **grace** *of God, for if righteousness comes through the* **Law**, *then Christ died needlessly.* (Galatians 2:21, emphasis mine)

> *You have been severed from Christ, you who are seeking to be justified by* **law**: *you have fallen from* **grace**. (Galatians 5:4, emphasis mine)

Before we continue, let us look again at a passage that we have previously quoted:

> *But when the fullness of time came, God sent forth His Son, born of a woman, born under the Law, so that He might redeem those who were under the Law, that we might receive the adoption as sons.* (Galatians 4:4-5)

We have already discussed the fact that Jesus came to fulfill the Law. In other words, by the time He came out of the grave, not only did He win the game, He owned the game. It was done! No more contest! He mastered every nuance of the knowledge of good and evil and came out victorious. Now that the Law had been fulfilled, there was something else that needed to be released on the earth in order for mankind to live in freedom. From the scriptures we have just quoted, it is clear that the unlikely antidote to the Law was none other than grace: the historical zenith of love, poured out at the cross in order to set us free from the condition that had held us captive since the first bite of the forbidden fruit.

A Definition of Grace

It is interesting to think of the contrast between law and grace and we are going to explore this difference. Before we do, however, let us try and come to a good definition of grace. There is much controversy over this subject, and I believe that much of it comes from a misunderstanding of the meaning of grace. The New Testament Greek word for grace is "charis." It is the same root word that we get "charismatic" from. Here is a description of the word as given in Strong's Concordance:

> **Charis,** *khar'-ece;* from *5463; graciousness* (as *gratifying),* of manner or act (abstr. or concr.: lit., fig. or spiritual: espec. the divine influence upon the heart, and

its reflection in the life; including *gratitude*):—acceptable, benefit, favor, gift, grace (-ious), joy, liberality, pleasure, thank (-s,-worthy). [1]

The standard, traditional definition of grace is "unmerited favor," but as we can easily see, this description is only part of the story. Here is what grace is in the New Testament: it is a divine influence or empowerment released upon our hearts and reflected into our lives, making us acceptable before God, allowing us to live under favor, to have heavenly benefits and gifts, to be joyful, to experience pleasure, and to enjoy all of the liberality that heaven has to offer. To think that this indescribable gift was released at the cross is beyond comprehension. It is also interesting to consider how "grace" would contrast with "law."

With this concept in mind, there is one popular vein of thought I would like to mention. I have had a lot of contact with people who view grace as a sin-covering agent. I hear them say such things as, "Whatever I do, grace has me covered." This is somewhat of an erroneous definition. Although a bit controversial, I would like to say that grace is not really a sin covering agent, the blood of Jesus is. In other words, the blood of Jesus covers and erases sin (and yes, this covering is completely free and available to anyone who will ask). On the other hand, grace empowers us to live on a completely different plain; a lifestyle free from the grip of sin and the Law.

I would also like to point out that grace flourishes in an environment of truth: "grace and truth" were realized in Jesus Christ. For this reason, if we are in a situation where there is no truth (or limited truth), grace will have a difficult time bringing closure, healing, and victory. Instead, law will usurp authority, demanding condemnation and punishment. In contrast, full and unconditional truth releases us (John 8:32, "sets us free") into a milieu of grace.

> *Grace flourishes in an environment of truth: "grace and truth" were realized in Jesus Christ.*

Let us now follow through with our thought process. If the cross is the reincarnated tree of life, then it would stand to reason that "grace" would be the fruit of the tree of life; a divine empowerment released to give us life again, transform us, and point us in a completely different direction from the pathways of good and evil. This transition of thought was difficult in the days of the early church because the system of law was so entrenched in daily Jewish life, customs, and religious traditions. Reading through the New Testament epistles, we find much of the energy the Apostle Paul focused on sorting out this new "grace" lifestyle.

However, today the battle is no less challenging because we as humans are drawn to law faster than a speeding bullet. As previously mentioned, we have little idea what to do with freedom, and our default is to start adding restrictions in order to keep us from doing wrong (in other words, evil). Once we start down this road, we are well on our way to "falling from grace." Some of these issues can be a bit contentious, but we are not going to let that stop us from exploring them. What is at stake here is the type of freedom that can elevate us to new apexes of liberty, authority, friendship with God, and enjoyment of life on this planet. This kind of freedom allows us to live with one foot on the earth and the other in heaven.

Contrasting Lifestyles

Let us start unraveling some of this mystery by contrasting a few characteristics of the two systems: law and grace. First, by wide definition, law is a legal system of rights and wrongs with rewards for doing good things, and consequences for doing the wrongs. Grace, on the other hand, is a God-given influence or empowerment reflected into our lives that has everything to do with a relationship. The power of grace is released through the cross, as an overflow of this relationship, enabling us to do good instinctively rather than obsessing over matters of good and evil. Law can easily be done without a relationship with God, grace cannot. As we will see, law and grace are not really opposites; they are two totally different ways of doing life. With this in mind, here are some contrasting statements revealing the difference between the two systems:

> *L*aw and grace are not really opposites; they are two totally different ways of doing life.

Law - a system based on the fruit of the tree of knowledge of good and evil.

Grace - an empowerment based on the fruit of the tree of life.

Law - a system of life based on beating the curse.

Grace - an empowerment of life based on the blessing as given in the garden.

Law - a system of endless rules and regulations.

Grace - an empowerment of endless freedom.

Law - a system where rules are written on stone and parchment.

Grace - an empowerment where a new law is written invisibly on our hearts.

Law - a system based on the fear of punishment.

Grace - an empowerment based on relationship and friendship.

Law - a system of self-examination.

Grace - an empowerment from keeping our eyes on Jesus.

Law - a system where we look at the wrong in our lives.

Grace - an empowerment to look at the beauty given to us at the cross.

Law - a system of trying to stay away from evil.

Grace - an empowerment to effortlessly transform into the image of Jesus.

Law - a system where people are slaves and servants.

Grace - an empowerment that makes us sons and daughters.

Law - a system of striving for our redemption.

Grace - an empowerment of resting in the finished work of the cross.

Law - a system of being judged and receiving condemnation.

Grace - an empowerment of freedom where there is nothing to judge.

Law - a system where we work for everything we get in life.

Grace - an empowerment of effortlessly bearing fruit in love, faith, and rest.

Law - a system where good will happen if we keep rules.

Grace - an empowerment where good will happen because of what Jesus has done.

Law - a system where we are guided by a tutor (the Law).

Grace - an empowerment where we are led by the Spirit.

Law - a system based on doing things in our own strength.

Grace - an empowerment where we can effortlessly do things in His strength.

Law - a system of trying to achieve a standard but never quite measuring up.

Grace - an empowerment to effortlessly achieve an even higher standard.

The First Struggle

Let us go back to the beginning once more. It now becomes evident that the very first life-changing choice or struggle in the garden was actually a struggle between law and grace. Adam and Eve were free. They had uninterrupted union and relationship with God. They were living under a grace-influenced environment; the empowerment of blessing of Almighty God as declared by His first words to them. In this condition there was no need for them to look at themselves. They were not even self-aware enough to notice that they were

> *The very first lifechanging choice or struggle in the garden was actually a struggle between law and grace.*

naked, albeit they were likely sporting a pretty stylish covering of glory over their bodies. But they were restless, and thought God was holding out on them. There was a commandment lurking in the shadows in the middle of the garden not to eat from a tree, and they no doubt wondered why God would withhold this fruit from them. In the end, when the serpent tempted them, rather than keeping their eyes on their God and eating from the tree of life, they chose to look in the other direction. As a result, they inadvertently abandoned their grace-freedom for law. It is little wonder the first thing they did was notice themselves. They immediately began to feel the weight and shame of their inadequacies. They also knew they were in danger of being judged and started to fear. So, they hid from the presence of God among the leaves. The question I pose is: when will we ever learn how to be free?

Where is Able, Your Brother?

The first murder on record was also a struggle between law and grace. Cain brought fruit as a sacrifice and tried to offer it up to God. This is fundamental to human nature. To this day we still try to bring fruit in an effort to be approved by God, thinking that the fruit of our lives (or the good things we have done) will make us acceptable in His eyes. We work day and night striving to do great, important things, and trying to avoid doing evil things. In the end, we feel good about ourselves, and try to offer this to God in exchange for our redemption as slaves—when all God ever wanted was a family. When Cain saw that God did not accept his offering, his countenance fell, and God told him sin was lurking at the door. The truth is, every time we try to offer the fruit of our lives in exchange for approval, sin is the result. Subconsciously this interchange drives us to do the very things we do not want to do. This approach is an endless spiral of missing the mark.

Abel, on the other hand, brought a blood sacrifice, which was accepted by God. Somehow we never seem to learn that the only way to be accepted in God's presence is through the blood of Jesus, end of story, book closed! Cain became jealous of Abel—an archetypical behavioral pattern still to this day. Those who try to establish a relationship with God based on works, or the fruit of their lives (as good as they might be), often persecute those pursuing a lifestyle of freedom. In the end, this post-garden confrontation became the context for the first human blood to be shed on the earth.

Let it be said here, most people heartily agree in theory with a statement such as, "The cross changed everything." They concur that the cross changed much, but as soon as it comes to law and traditions, the lines are drawn and judgment is handed down. There is also one consistent and loud complaint levied against those who desire to live a free and grace empowered lifestyle, found in this one question: "If you extend full grace to someone [sometimes called "greasy grace" by those who would find fault], are you not giving them a blanket license to sin?" There is a second, similar question that I have heard a lot: "What about repentance? Is it not important to constantly review our lives, find the hidden faults, and repent of them in order to keep a clean heart before God?" We are going to delve into these and other important issues in the upcoming pages.

---

1. James Strong, *A Concise Dictionary of the Words in the Greek Testament*, in *Strong's Exhaustive Concordance: Compact Edition* (Grand Rapids: Baker Book House, 1985), 77.

Chapter 7
What Has Changed?

Let us review one more time in detail our makeup as a human creation and how it relates to our world and redemption. We are a three part being consisting of a spirit, soul, and body (1 Thessalonians 5:23). At the beginning of time all three of these parts were free and integral to life. Our heavenly Father made us to co-exist in two realms simultaneously. Our spirit was made to interface with the heavenly or spiritual realm, and our bodies were made to interface with the earthly realm. Our soul and mind were created as the "in between" mechanism to draw these two worlds together, to give consciousness, and to make sense out of our existence.

Spirit, Soul, and Body

Our spirit was connected to God and alive through the Spirit of God who lived in us. It was the driving force of our being. Everything flowed from heaven into our spirit, into our soul to bring conscious expression, into our bodies, and then out into the physical world. This condition is referred to as being "spirit-led." Our souls were engaged and ruled by our spirits, and our minds were massive God-soaking-up organs. They would take information from the spirit realm and relay it to our bodies, and vice versa.

Our bodies were meticulously crafted to an almost unfathomable standard. They were beautiful, imbued with the glory of heaven, and in full agreement with our spirits, which were connected directly to God. I have heard it said that the best type of interface for any technology is one that the user hardly realizes is there. It is, in essence, invisible. In the beginning, such were our bodies. They offered such a seamless integration into our world that Adam and Eve didn't even realize they were naked. On top of that, nothing could penetrate the covering of glory and regeneration that was present in the garden. Even after the fall, this regenerative force was so significant there are many biblical records of humans living for almost 1000 years. There was perfect harmony among these three parts of our being, and it created

> *I*n the beginning there was perfect harmony among all three parts of our being, and it created a stunning symmetry of life in the first persons to live on our planet.

a stunning symmetry of life in the first persons to live on our planet.

All Areas Affected

After the fall, all areas of life were affected. The spirit of man became dead rather than alive, and became separated from his Maker (Isaiah 59:2). The Spirit of God, unable to live in an unholy environment, had to subsequently "vacate the premises" (Romans 8:9). The soul and mind became depraved and fallen (Titus 1:15-16). The mind chose to focus on ungodly things, so it took on a life of its own and began to side with the worldly part of the fallen man. The body took a massive hit. Separated from the life-giving force of the spirit, devoid of the fruit of the tree of life, and now connected to a cursed world, things got out of hand in a hurry. All of the natural and beautiful functions of the body turned into occasions for sin, and these appetites took on a life of their own. The sin-nature moved into the body and became the driving force of man rather than his spirit. In some places in the Bible, it is now called the "body of sin," the "old self," or sometimes the "flesh."

> *Knowing this, that our **old self** was crucified with Him, in order that our **body of sin** might be done away with, so that we would no longer be slaves to sin.* (Romans 6:6, emphasis mine)

*For while we were **in the flesh**, the sinful passions, which were aroused by the Law, were at work in the members of our body to bear fruit for death.* (Romans 7:5, emphasis mine)

The dead spirit, fallen soul, and sin-natureinhabited body is a horrific combination. When this triple menace is given jurisdiction over an individual, the result is a living environment devoid of hope.

Notice how these verses say that the sinful passions were at work in the members of our body. The sin-nature resides in our earthly body, and it is passed on from person to person each time a new life is conceived. The dead spirit, fallen soul, and sin-nature-inhabited body is a horrific combination. When this triple menace is given jurisdiction over an individual, the result is a living environment devoid of hope.

Now let us consider the condition of a born-again person under the New Covenant. Though there is much controversy over this subject, we will try to unravel a bit of it. I am not pointing fingers or judging anybody with these next words: I am speaking to myself, as it has taken me the best years of my life to discover any freedom I now walk in. However, be warned that we are after a few sacred cows.

Most evangelical Christians will agree that at the moment of new birth, the spirit of the person is made alive and the Spirit of God once again takes up residence inside of them. Here is where the general agreement stops. Many Christians believe that the other two parts of a person must, from this moment on, undergo a lifetime of endless work, which will not be completed until their entrance into heaven.

Stuck-in-the-Middle Soul

The most popular view of this scenario is as follows: while the spirit is instantly transformed, connecting and drawing us once more upward toward God, the body is left untouched by redemption. Because of the body's connection to the fallen and cursed world, it is constantly dragging and drawing us toward evil and "fleshly" practices. The soul is stuck in the middle, left to make the decision whether or not we will go God's way or the way of the flesh. "The Ways," by John Oxenham, is a poem that describes this way of thinking perfectly:

> *To every man there openeth*
> *A Way, and Ways, and a Way,*
> *And the High Soul climbs the High Way,*
> *And the Low Soul gropes the Low,*
> *And in between, on the misty flats,*
> *The rest drift to and fro.*

But to every man there openeth
A High Way, and a Low.
And every man decideth
The Way his soul shall go.[1]

This scenario lends itself to the idea that as we renew our mind with the things of God, and as we submit our wills to Him, our souls will gradually side more readily with our spirits in defeating the "fleshly" practices in our lives. As we move towards this paradigm, we become more "Christ-like," more pleasing to God, more holy, and more apt to stay away from sin. This constant "soul renovation" is often called "sanctification," and is seen as a lifelong process in most circles.

However, should a person start to neglect giving attention to his or her spirit's/soul's renewal/sanctification process, the balance will quickly begin to shift from the spirit back to the "fleshly" nature. The person will eventually sin habitually and end up "backslidden." This process can, in extreme situations, result in the eventual loss of the salvation of the person and upon death, their departure to hell rather than heaven—especially for those adhering to an Arminian theological mindset. Keep in mind in this scenario, the body (at least in this earthly lifetime) is considered primarily as a fallen and unredeemable part of our makeup, as well as the source of the "fleshly" desires we must fight for the rest of our lives. The only positive attribute given to the body in some instances is that there is provision made by Jesus at the cross for it to be healed from sickness and disease. However, most of the time, even though we will pray and ask for infirmity to be removed, the outcome is left up to the "will of God," and if the sickness is not removed it is considered divine providence.

There is much logic to this model of redemption, and those who adhere to it will defend it tooth and nail. There is a nod given to grace as "unmerited favor" in this system because we are unworthy of the gift of salvation that we are given, and subsequently we need God's grace. There is also a nod given to the fact that we cannot accomplish the task of defeating our sinful nature on our own, thus we are in need of God's grace and strength.

Theology of Repentance

There is room for an elaborate theology of repentance in this worldview, and it is touted as the primary tool in humanity's ongoing struggle against sin and the transformation of the individual. Repentance is coupled with a posture of constant self-examination, and a daily discipline of studying the Bible. These activities are done in hopes that our soul will agree more readily with our spirit and, by extrapolation, the will of God.

There have been many volumes written by ancient mystics about the fight with the body, or the flesh. Some of them go into great detail about elaborate times of fasting, prayer, and self-discipline. I recall one story where a monk, when faced with the temptation of a beautiful woman sleeping in the next room of his tent, burned his fingers down to the bone with a candle to avoid giving in to, or even thinking about, his fleshly desires. Some of these poor souls went to great lengths attempting to stay away from the evil in the world, isolating themselves and doing extreme things.

This model I have described is the life experience of the majority of born-again persons I have met, and, until recently, it has also been the basis of my own life experience. There is good reason for someone to buy into this way of thinking. It fits comfortably with the way most of us seem to struggle against sin, and it is assumed as basic foundational doctrine in much of today's Church culture. There are some wonderfully sincere and godly people who believe this theology, and most of them will argue that it is also the basis for revival in a country, city, or church.

The premise here is that we, even as Christians, are flawed and sin-ridden because our fleshly nature is still fully intact and powerful. For this reason there are many sins that we commit on a daily and momentary basis, which we don't even know about. These infractions include sins of "omission," such as failing to tell the truth, etc. There are also sins of the mind, such as pride, jealousy, and looking at someone in lust. Then there are the big "in your face" sins of "commission," such as stealing, cheating, lying, and adultery. The assumption is that because we are constantly committing these sins, we slip quite low on the scale of holiness, and God cannot be in partnership with unrighteousness.

The only thing that can get us closer to God's holiness again is to realize, own up to, and repent of the sin. In this scenario, there is often much emphasis on emotion and "godly sorrow." For the most part, it is assumed that if a person deeply repents of sin, and feels much godly sorrow, the result will be a longer lasting, life-changing moment that will set the person on a higher track of holiness for a long time. Part of this experience is feeling the weight or ugliness of the sin to such a degree that we will think twice before doing the same thing again. We are also sincerely sorry for disappointing our Lord and putting Him through more agony on the cross for our sake. This repentance process becomes stamped in our mind as a signpost; an unpleasant place we hope to stay away from in the future.

If a whole group of people come to God in this way, repent of their sin, and return to "true holiness," their actions supposedly create a gateway that a holy God can enter to partner with man and accomplish His will on the earth. The resulting refreshment sought here is called "revival," and it is prayed for as a welcome contrast to the dryness we often experience in our spiritual journey.

Some Familiar Scriptures

With this scenario in mind, let us now look at some familiar scripture verses and see how this paradigm fits with the Word of God. This is a bit of a long list, but bear with me as we allow the word of God to speak to us.

Therefore if anyone is in Christ, he is a new creature; the old things passed away; behold, new things have come. [Some translations say, "all things have become new."] (2 Corinthians 5:17)

Knowing this, that our old self was crucified with Him, in order that our body of sin might be done away with, so that we would no longer be slaves to sin. (Romans 6:6)

For while we were in the flesh, the sinful passions, which were aroused by the Law, were at work in the members of our body to bear fruit for death. But now we have been released from the Law, having died to that by which we were bound, so that we serve in the newness of the Spirit and not in the oldness of the letter. (Romans 7:5-6)

For what the Law could not do, weak as it was through the flesh, God did; sending His own Son in the likeness of sinful flesh and as an offering for sin, He condemned sin in the flesh. (Romans 8:3)

However, you are not in the flesh but in the Spirit if indeed the Spirit of God dwells in you. (Romans 8:9)

Therefore I urge you, brethren, by the mercies of God, to present your bodies a living and holy sacrifice, acceptable to God, which is your spiritual service of worship. (Romans 12:1)

Or do you not know that your body is a temple of the Holy Spirit who is in you, whom you have from God, and that you are not your own? For you have been bought with a price; therefore glorify God in your body. (1 Corinthians 6:19-20)

[This passage speaks of the light of the knowledge of the glory of God in the face of Christ] *But we have this treasure in earthen vessels, so that the surpassing greatness of the power will be of God and not from ourselves.* (2 Corinthians 4:7)

I have been crucified with Christ; and it is no longer I who live, but Christ lives in me; and the life which I now live in the flesh I live by faith in the Son of God, who loved me and gave Himself up for me. (Galatians 2:20)

Christian Foundations

Now that we have read through these passages, let us talk about a few basic things. I view these points as foundational and essential to the understanding of our Christian faith. There is one underlying theme that weaves a common thread throughout all of these verses. I will make this point bluntly and without apology: friends, in the new birth our old sinful nature is dead! I will say it once more, in a slightly different way.

> *We have been made brand new in nature—spirit, soul, and body! End of story!*

We do not have a renewed spirit, a sinful, dirty body, and a lost-in-the-middle soul. We have been made brand new in nature—spirit, soul, and body! End of story! The first verse quoted here states if we are in Christ, we have become a new creature. The J. B. Phillips translation reads, "he becomes a new person altogether." The old has passed away, *all* things have become new. This *"all"* includes our bodies.

Let us look at another scenario: there is absolutely no way the Holy Spirit could live inside a sin-nature inhabited, fallen body. This condition is the very reason He had to leave in the first place back in the garden. If the cross didn't return us to a position where our bodies are holy and pure, how could the Holy Spirit take up residence inside of us again, calling us His "temple" of all things? Some will claim this is possible because He actually resides in our spirit and not our body. However, if the body is His temple or house, He lives there. My point is that our spirits reside inside our bodies and His Spirit does the same. Second Corinthians 4:6-7 states we have a treasure in our earthen vessel: the "glory of God as seen in the face of Christ." If our bodies are still inhabited by sin-nature, how could this glory reside in us? One thing I know about the glory is it burns up anything not holy, so if we believe our bodies are sinful and flawed, most of us would be good and crispy right now.

How about the verse that tells us to present our bodies as a living sacrifice, holy and acceptable to God (Romans 12:1)? If our bodies are still unholy or blemished, there is no way this sacrifice could be accepted by God. If you look back at the numerous sacrificial references in the Old Testament, the only acceptable sacrifice was a flawless, unblemished, "very best you have" sacrifice.

Then there are the verses which state that our body of sin has been done away with, and verses which talk in the past tense about our condition, "when we were in the flesh," saying that we now serve in a new and living way. Romans 8:2 clearly states that Jesus "condemned sin in the flesh." He killed it. It is dead and gone. When He went down into that grave, we went with Him because we were "in Him." We were crucified with Him on that cross—spirit, soul, and body. There are many more of these types of verses throughout the New Testament, but they all communicate the same basic message. Jesus came to make us new and He didn't do a half job, only redeeming our spirit, and leaving us to fight against the soul and flesh for the rest of our lives. He did it all: He redeemed us spirit, soul, and body.

The Reappearance of Good and Evil

So where does this leave us in regard to our subject of "good and evil" versus "life," "law" versus "grace?" Notice that the theology of a renewed spirit, sin-ridden body, and lost-in-the-middle soul is fully contingent on one thing: the knowledge of good and evil. Once again we are trying to do good and stay away from evil. The main entrée on this menu is called "sin-consciousness." This notion means that we are constantly aware of sin (evil) we are doing, and we try our best to stay away from it. We are acutely afraid that we might be committing sin we don't even know about, so we go on periodic digging expeditions to find and expunge the unintentional sin via repentance. If this is the best situation Jesus could leave us in as far as redemption is concerned, why did He even go to the cross? We are left in nearly the same condition as back in the days of the Law.

There is probably no more destructive force in a person's life than a perpetual "sin-consciousness," and it is also very unappealing to God. Imagine for an instant if you had a child who was always in a corner crying and telling

> *The theology of a renewed spirit, sin-ridden body, and lost-in-the-middle soul is fully contingent on one thing: the knowledge of good and evil.*

you how bad he or she had been. Then imagine again if this child would constantly look for even the smallest bad thing they had done and tell you about it. This situation would get old very quickly. There is no relationship-killer like being sin-conscious. There is no healthy friendship, family, or marriage on ground earth that could be built on this foundation. Instead, the relationship would end up being codependent, dysfunctional, and abusive. How do we think a relationship with our heavenly Father could be any different?

A Vital Question

These thoughts bring up another noteworthy query: if we really have been made new in nature—spirit, soul, and body, how is it that sin still darkens our lives so easily? It is a fair question; one that kept me on the side of law rather than grace for many years. Most of my life, I supposed the source of sin to be an ever-existent, dominant sin-nature constantly dragging me down. This concept, in retrospect, was some-what comforting to me. When I would do something wrong, my con-science could be eased with such inner negotiations as: "Hey Dean, give yourself a break—we have a sin-nature to defeat here!" Once this factor was removed from the equation, I had a hard time imagining from where else sin might come. However, remember that even without a sin-nature—in a state of complete innocence, Adam and Eve sinned. Consequently, through many hours of meditation and pondering on this subject, I have come to the realization that sin originates from the exact opposite place I once assumed it came from. In the life of a New Testament

> *I*n the life of a New Testament believer, sin proceeds from looking at, and trying to keep law, not an intrinsic, rogue sin-nature.

believer, sin proceeds from looking at, and trying to keep law, not an intrinsic, rogue sin-nature.

If we hold up the governing knowledge of good and evil (the Law), putting it before our eyes; the very knowledge of wrong puts thought into our minds. This progression, in turn, gives power to sin, bringing it forth in our lives, and releasing death upon us (James 1:14-15). The writings of the Apostle Paul are very specific in this regard:

> *By the works of the Law no flesh will be justified in His sight; for through the Law comes the knowledge of sin.* (Romans 3:20)

> *The sting of death is sin, and the power of sin is the Law.* (1 Corinthians 15:56)

Even in a state of everything being made new by Christ, if we focus our attention on trying to keep law (trying to be good), it can empower an imitation of that old nature so fast we will wonder what hit us. It will put us in a tailspin; a never-ending cycle of sin, guilt, condemnation, tears, repentance, and powerlessness. This conundrum is the very situation the devil got us into that kept us bound for thousands of years. It makes logical sense that he would want us to believe we are still sin-nature-ridden even if we are not. Only here can the accuser keep us defeated rather than victorious, free, and supernaturally orientated. There is a passage in Galatians that speaks about this concept:

> *Nevertheless knowing that a man is not justified by the works of the Law but through faith in Christ Jesus, even we have believed in Christ Jesus, so that we may be justified by faith in Christ and not by the works of the Law; since by the works of the Law no flesh will be justified. But if, while seeking to be justified in Christ, we ourselves have also been found sinners, is Christ then a minister of sin? May it never be! For if I rebuild what I have once destroyed, I prove myself to be a transgressor.* (Galatians 2:16-18)

Although a bit wordy, this passage tells us we are not justified by the Law but through faith in Christ Jesus. It also says that while seeking to be justified in Christ we can become sinners again. It goes on to tell us that if we rebuild what we have once destroyed, we prove to be a transgressor. So what is it that we have destroyed? In the context of these verses it is the Law. Accordingly, if we go back to living by law once we have been freed from its influence, it can pull us back into sin quite easily. We are, in essence, returned to a situation where even though we are no longer under the Law, our old life under the Law is imitated, causing transgression in our life.

Condemnation or the Holy Spirit?

I have watched countless people in my lifetime, myself included, struggle with sin. We will inevitably try to repent—only to be drawn, as if with an imaginary rubber band, back to the same old patterns. Having attended numerous Christian gatherings, there is an all-too-common routine I have experienced. At the end, there is a challenge to the congregants to have a moment of self-examination of some kind, followed by a period of repentance or resolve to "do better in certain areas." These introspective targets can range in scope from "good" subjects, such as praying more, to matters of "evil," such as casting down pride, but they all generate the same basic result. People feel bad about themselves, and then resolve, by some form of repentance or self-discipline, to try and make improvements in the areas they have deemed themselves deficient. It is also unfortunate that the ones with the softest, most beautiful hearts often feel the worst. They leave the place of meeting feeling deeply moved, but eventually sink back down to the same, or an even lower level of attainment than before.

This condition is what the Bible calls "condemnation," but in many circles, sadly, it is seen as an act of the Holy Spirit convicting or bringing correction. However, make no mistake; what has happened is that we have looked at the Law, found that we are not measuring up to its standard, been judged as guilty, condemned for our actions, and told to do better. There is a self-governed appeal to this approach that is so subtle it is almost frightening. Yet, in my opinion, the hardest pill to swallow is the fact that this system produces the very opposite result of what we are trying to accomplish. We stand a bit straighter for a while, but slump down lower than ever in the end. It is the way our human nature works. Looking at sin or suggesting someone might be a sinner is not the way to proliferate victory in a person's life. Sometimes I wonder if we didn't have this formula, what we would do with our time. There have been many years of my life when I was given 52 ways I did not quite measure up.

> *Looking at sin or suggesting someone might be a sinner is not the way to proliferate victory in a person's life.*

There is no life in this approach because the very thing we are trying to free ourselves from is the very thing we are looking at. The result: when we look at sin, we reap sin in our lives. After eating from this tree, if we look at ourselves, we will always see nakedness in some form or another. What did Adam and Eve do in the garden? First they looked at the tree, then they ate from the tree, then they started to look at themselves. They saw that they were naked, and they hid from the presence of God. This chain of events has proven to be our Achilles heel from the beginning. The focus of our eyes, directing us to subsequent action, is our weakest human characteristic.

This understanding is essential to living a sin-free lifestyle. Once we understand the true origin of sin, we can finally get a grip on how it works and then rescind its influence over our lives. If we believe it comes from inside us—even from our very nature, we will forever be fighting against ourselves. This practice leads to an extremely arduous way of doing life: one inundated with shadow boxing, burnout, and cyclical defeat. There is a virtual prison in the sin-nature-ridden mindset for a believer in Christ. On the other hand, if we realize that sin comes from looking at and trying to keep law, then all we need to do is stay away from law, focus our attention instead on the tree of life, and let the influence of grace propel us into a life of freedom!

Many will criticize those in a "grace movement" for allegedly having free license to sin, but the truth is: sin is empowered and multiplied by the Law, whereas grace, if applied properly, will enable us to soar above this entire scenario. I have learned that there is only one way to look at one's self—through the eyes of Jesus and through the lens of being "in Christ." With this view, we can't even see the sin because He has no sin and we are in Him.

There has to be something better than an "old-nature-ridden," sin-conscious mindset in store for a born-again person, and it is found in a welcome passage in Romans 7. Here Paul is talking about how his old life under the system of law looked, and he makes an extremely "tweet worthy" statement:

> *Wretched man that I am! Who will set me free from the body of this death?* ***Thanks be to God through Jesus Christ our Lord!*** (Romans 7:24-25, emphasis mine)

In Jesus we have been freed from our old sinful nature. This shift in thought is such good news. Now that we have torn down some religious paradigms, we are going to take the next pages to carefully and deliberately rebuild our entire redemption the "grace" way. Grab on to your seats, we are about to kick in the afterburners!

---

1. William Arthur Dunkerley, *All's Well* (New York: George H. Doran, 1916), 91.

Chapter 8
The Extreme New Birth

So exactly how does the new birth work? What did Jesus do for us on the cross? What is the extent of our redemption? Was Jesus really able to take us back to garden conditions again? In order to answer these questions, we are going to take a look at some of the text of Romans 8.

Before we do, however, let us look at a couple of words that often co-exist in Scripture passages speaking about our salvation: faith and grace. We find them in the same verse several times in the New Testament. To understand the new birth, it is essential to grasp how these two redemptive concepts interact with each other. In an effort to get a handle on this, we will sample a few of these verses in the books of Ephesians and Romans.

But God, being rich in mercy, because of His great love with which He loved us, even when we were dead in our transgressions, made us alive together with Christ (by grace you have been saved). (Ephesians 2:4-5, empha-sis mine)

For by **grace** *you have been saved through* **faith***; and that not of yourselves, it is the gift of God.* (Ephesians 2:8, emphasis mine)

Therefore, having been justified by **faith***, we have peace with God through our Lord Jesus Christ, through whom also we have obtained our introduction by* **faith** *into this* **grace** *in which we stand; and we exult in hope of the glory of God.* (Romans 5:1-2, emphasis mine)

The first two verses speak directly about our new birth; stating clearly that we have been saved by grace. The next verse repeats that we have been saved by grace, but this time it adds, "through faith." Romans 5 then gives us a bit more insight on exactly how this works: we gain our introduction into grace by faith.

So what happens when we choose the Lord Jesus Christ as our Savior? The first thing we need to do is to believe. This action requires faith, and it starts a chain reaction in our spirit, soul, and body. The moment faith is released, grace is acti-vated—it is, "by grace, through faith." This process is always the way it works with things provided for us on the cross. First we believe; then the faith releases the empowerment of grace to accomplish what we have believed for. Let's remember what grace is: a divine influence or empowerment released upon our hearts and reflected into our lives through the broken body and blood of Jesus. The first thing grace does is to saturate our spirit with resurrection power, instantly bringing our human spirit back to life. We are then reconnected to our Father God and the Holy Spirit re-inhabits our body, becoming one with our spirit.

So now that we have a brand new living spirit, the question remains: what happens to our soul and body? Romans chapters 5, 6, and 7 have a lot to say about this question, and one must read them through in their entirety to catch the context of what Paul is saying. I can tell you this: up until Romans 8, the majority of this text speaks of the body and the mind. It describes in great detail the process of the Law, how we came to be under it, how it works, and how the sin-nature interacts with our body of flesh to defeat us. We have talked much about this reality in the previous chapters, quoting many parts of Romans, but the exciting news really starts in Romans 8.

> *Therefore there is now no condemnation for those who are in Christ Jesus. For the law of the spirit of life in Christ Jesus has set you free from the law of sin and death. For what the Law could not do, weak as it was through the*

flesh, God did; sending His own Son in the likeness of sinful flesh and as an offering for sin, He condemned sin in the flesh. (Romans 8:1-3)

No More Sin-Nature

Notice there is suddenly a new law in place. Once our human spirit has become alive again, we are set free from the old law of sin and death by a new law called the "law of the spirit of life," and it is "in Christ Jesus." We will talk about this new law in upcoming pages. Then it goes on to tell us exactly how Jesus came to set us free, which is the best of news. You see, what the old Law was trying to do was put us in a position where we could be righteous; however, because of the weakness of the sin-nature in our flesh, it was never able to accomplish what it was intended to do. When Jesus went to the cross, He became the likeness of sinful flesh. In other words, He took on our old sin-nature. He offered his body up as a sacrifice, paid the price for our transgression, and condemned and killed sin in the flesh forever. And He did all of this while carrying us along for the ride, "in Him," so to speak. Once again, we have quoted many scriptures referring to this progression:

Knowing this, that our old self was crucified with Him, in order that our body of sin might be done away with, so that we would no longer be slaves to sin; for he who has died is freed from sin. (Romans 6:6-7)

Since the old self or old nature takes up residence in our bodies, this verity is awesome news. Our body of sin was crucified with Christ and died with Him, meaning that we no longer have a sin-nature! In the new birth, our spirit was made brand new by the power of grace; and then this same grace invaded our body and permeated it with resurrection life, purging it of the fallen sin-nature. Essentially, we have been returned to nearly the same condition we enjoyed back in the Garden of Eden. There is one difference; something we are still waiting for.

> *Our body of sin was crucified with Christ and died with Him, meaning that we no longer have a sin-nature.*

Our bodies have not yet been fully glorified and thus they are still mortal while living on this earth. The final fulfillment of this promise will not happen until we die and go to heaven. However, there is much good news to rejoice in, and our bodies have been given an additional boost that we will talk about shortly. Let's now continue with Romans 8:

For what the Law could not do, weak as it was through the flesh, God did; sending His own Son in the likeness of sinful flesh and as an offering for sin, He condemned sin in the flesh, so that the requirement of the Law might be fulfilled in us, who do not walk according to the flesh but according to the spirit. (Romans 8:3-4)

Our old nature has been crucified and killed so the requirement of the Law can now be fulfilled in us. It was part of the plan that we be righteous right from the beginning. We were never meant for evil, however, when we try to do good things on our own strength, we fail because we are looking at good and evil with our earthly eyes. The good news is that we have now been put in a position where we can finally fulfill the Law, or in other words, do good things without even trying. The reason: we are no longer being ruled by the sin-nature residing in our bodies or flesh. In other words, we are no longer walking "according to the flesh." We are now, once again, being ruled by our spirit; however, our human spirit is not the only one at work. The Holy Spirit is also with us, inextricably linked with our spirit, releasing a substance called grace, which enables us to effortlessly walk a higher road than the old Law could have imagined possible. There is a scripture in the Old Testament that speaks about this transformation, which was part of God's plan all along:

"Behold, days are coming," declares the Lord, "when I will make a new covenant with the house of Israel and with the

house of Judah." "This is the covenant which I will make with the house of Israel after those days," declares the Lord, "I will put My Law within them and on their heart I will write it; and I will be their God, and they shall be my people. They will not teach again, each man his neighbor, and each man his brother, saying, 'Know the Lord,' for they will all know Me, from the least of them to the greatest of them," declares the Lord, "for I will forgive their iniquity, and their sin I will remember no more." (Jeremiah 31:31, 33-34)

In the New Testament, the writer of Hebrews repeats this exact same narrative in Hebrews 8:7-13. This time, the end of the text declares that the New Covenant has made the Old Covenant obsolete. In order to understand where the new law of the "spirit of life in Christ Jesus" is written, we need to know where the old one was written. It was written in the stone of the Ten Commandments and the parchment contained in the first five books of the Bible, which Paul refers to as, "the letter."

> *But now we have been released from the Law, having died to that by which we were bound, so that we serve in newness of the spirit and not in the oldness of **the letter**.* (Romans 7:8, emphasis mine)

This commandment was written with "letters" and is the standard of the knowledge of good and evil that we have been trying to live up to for thousands of years. It is also called the Old Covenant, and in order to keep it, we need to look at it with our earthly, natural eyes. In fact in the Old Testament they were told to meditate on this Law day and night.

What God was saying in Jeremiah is there would be a New Covenant, and in this New Covenant there would still be a law, but it would be written invisibly on the inside of the hearts and spirits of His people. In this new system we no longer need to look at the Law because it is now indelibly and secretly written in a place where no human eye can see: in our hearts.

> *If you are under the impression that the life of grace gives you free license to sin, think again. The requirement of this new lifestyle is actually morally higher than the old.*

If you are under the impression that the life of grace gives you free license to sin, think again. The requirement of this new lifestyle is actually morally higher than the old. If you don't believe me, think for a moment about some of the statements Jesus made. Here is an example:

You have heard that it was said, "you shall not commit adultery;" but I say to you that everyone who looks at a woman with lust for her has already committed adultery with her in his heart. (Matthew 5:27-28)

Here we see the old Law setting a standard: "you shall not commit adultery." Then Jesus releases a new grace law establishing an even higher standard. Now, consider this statement by Paul:

What then? Shall we sin because we are not under the Law but under grace? May it never be! (Romans 6:15)

Does "Effortless" Really Exist?

This part gets some people really upset. Because of the empowerment of grace released in our lives, we are able to meet this new standard effortlessly! This new law of grace is quite invisible. Because it is written inside our hearts, we couldn't even look at it if we wanted to, and God has done it this way for good reason. There is only one place we should have had our eyes focused: on the tree of life. If we try to focus on external laws we will fail. However, if we fix our eyes on Jesus who is the light of the world and sink our whole being into the pursuit of His presence, the empowerment of grace will enable us to meet this new requirement instinctively and without striving. Consequently, we will find ourselves in a divine condition of relationship, rest, fellowship, and freedom! He who the Son has set free is free indeed (John 8:36). An Old Testament psalmist was on to something when writing, "Thy word have I hid in my heart so I might not sin against Thee" (Psalm 119:11). Even back then, when steeped in law, this poet knew the key to living a lifestyle free from sin was not trying to keep the Law, but having the Law "hidden" on the inside of the heart. When it comes to law— out of sight, and out of mind is the only way to be successful.

Let's continue on with the narrative of Romans 8. The next set of verses tells us those who walk according to the flesh set their mind on the flesh. However, those who walk according to the Spirit set their mind on the things of the Spirit. Here we see the mention of our soul-realm. Once the sin-nature is dead, our minds are free to focus on the things of the spirit because we are now ruled by our spirit rather than our flesh. There is one key verse in the middle of this section that brings total freedom from fear and concern about the old nature:

> *However, you are not in the flesh but in the Spirit, if indeed the Spirit of God dwells in you. But if anyone does not have the Spirit of Christ, he does not belong to Him.* (Romans 8:9)

To ease the troubled mind of anyone who might still be wondering if they have an old fleshly nature we need only ask one question: "Does the Spirit of God dwell in you?" If He does, then you are no longer in the flesh! End of story. Let's continue.

> *If Christ is in you, though the body is dead because of sin, yet the spirit is alive because of righteousness. But if the Spirit of Him who raised Jesus from the dead dwells in you, He who raised Christ Jesus from the dead will also give life to your mortal bodies through His Spirit who dwells in you.* (Romans 8:10-11)

Good News for our Bodies

These verses give some of the best news yet. If the Spirit who raised Jesus from the dead dwells in you, He will give life to your mortal body. Once again, does the Spirit dwell in you? If He does, then the body that became dead when it was crucified with Christ (and the sin-nature was taken out of it) is put in an exciting new position. The same Spirit who brought your human spirit back to life and made you righteous will also infuse your mortal body with life. In other words, the work of the cross neutralized our bodies as far as the sin-nature is concerned, and now the Holy Spirit, if allowed, can actually re-energize them. There is a world of freedom, bodily restoration, and physical healing hidden in this portion of scripture. In my opinion, there are few who understand and believe this amazing promise enough to tap into it. I will often sit and wait on the Holy Spirit, specifically asking Him to permeate me with this life. I then rest in His presence, allowing time for Him to work in my body. My wife has a nightly ritual of inviting the Holy Spirit to infil-

> *The same Spirit who brought your human spirit back to life and made you righteous will also infuse your mortal body with life.*

trate her body, going in and out of every cell, tissue, and vital organ. She then waits, praying in the Spirit as He does His work. Together, we view this discipline as much part of the mainte-nance of our earthly bodies as eating well, exercising, and resting. Most believers go through life with a view that their bodies are a necessary evil on this earth. In fact, the opposite could not be truer. Our bodies are the temple of the Holy Spirit, set apart, sanctified, made holy, and injected with the very glory of heaven.

Who are we - Really?

Let me tell you exactly who you are in Christ: you are a born-again, blood-washed, innocent human being with a vibrantly alive spirit intertwined with the Spirit of God. You have a body that is pure and beautiful, completely purged of its old sin-nature, flooded with resurrection-life, ready to do the bidding of the spirit / Holy Spirit. The law of God has been written invisibly on the pages of your heart, allowing you to live a life free of sin and the curse effortlessly. You also have a mind that can be renewed daily; ready and willing to help your spirit-ruled being release the kingdom of God on this earth.

Family Identity

The next few verses in Romans 8 tell us that by the Spirit the works of the flesh are put to death. Then the narrative starts to talk about another element of our redemption: our sonship and our inheritance.

> *For all who are being led by the Spirit of God, these are the sons of God. For you have not received a spirit of slavery leading to fear again, but you have received the spirit of adoption as sons by which we cry out, "Abba Father." The Spirit Himself testifies with our spirit that we are children of God.* (Romans 8:14-16)

What our Father God wanted right from the beginning was a family. The potential for the joint family venture of bringing earth under the dominion of the kingdom of heaven is the very reason He made us in His image and likeness.

When we chose the knowledge of good and evil, and subsequently law over relationship in His family, we became a planet full of orphans. Each one of us was disconnected from God the Father. We then became the property of a cruel, foreign taskmaster: the devil, and inadvertently opted for slavery rather than freedom and sonship. We might attain to the position of a servant under the Old Covenant ("Moses My **servant** is dead," Joshua 1:2, emphasis mine). However, even though this Old Testament title held great honor, it still fell short of a "grace empowered" family identity. Under the New Covenant, each one of us can "know" (Jeremiah 31) his or her God in a way that is only hinted at in the first two chapters of Genesis. We have now been restored to a relationship of family, friendship, and divine favor ("No longer do I call you servants, for a servant does not know what his master is doing; but I have called you **friends,**" John 15:15, NKJV, emphasis mine).

There is one more part of Romans 8 that I would like to look at before moving on. It sums everything up in a most beautiful way:

> *For those whom He foreknew, He also predestined to become conformed to the image of His Son, so that He would be the first born among many brethren; and these whom He predestined, He also called; and these whom He called, He*

also justified; and these whom He justified, He also glorified. What then shall we say to these things? If God is for us, who is against us! (Romans 8:29-31)

Notice how this text is written entirely in the past tense. The time for the fulfillment of these verses is now. Provision has already been made on the cross and we have been given an open invitation from heaven to explore the depths of these new-birth realities. First, we have been conformed to the image of Jesus. There is so much hidden meaning and freedom in this statement that it almost defies description. There is another similar passage in 1 John:

As He [Jesus] *is, so also are we in this world.* (1 John 4:17)

This declaration makes "normal life" absolutely impossible for a born-again person. To think that the resurrected Jesus was but the first prototype of many (we being the many) is mind blowing. But this is only the beginning. Let's read on. We have also been called, justified (made righteous), and glorified! Perhaps we are not as far away from the original

> *To think that the resurrected Jesus was but the first prototype of many (we being the many) is mind blowing.*

garden conditions as we thought. I know someday we will have fully glorified bodies, but my challenge to you today is: how far do you want to go? We know of stories in the Old Testament when Moses' face was shining so brightly with the glory of God that he had to put a veil over it—and these events took place under the Old Covenant!

Clothed with Fire

Then there is the story in Acts 2, when tongues of fire descended upon the disciples. What exactly do you think these glowing flames were? It was the glory of God resting upon them. So, after being suffused with resurrection power spirit, soul, and body, there is one more new-birth reality. With the "baptism in the Holy Spirit" experience, we are clothed with fire or glory on the outside. Think for a moment about being immersed in the Holy Spirit. Wow! This situation parallels the condition Jesus was in when He came out of His baptism. The Holy Spirit came as a dove and remained upon Him.

The first thing that happened after this event was a voice that spoke from heaven saying, "This is My beloved Son in whom I am well pleased" (Matthew 3:17). I invite you to hear this same phrase spoken over you by the Father. Most people will not venture to this place because they think they are unworthy; however, the Father is declaring this over you every day, even at this very moment. Hear His voice, and boldly receive these words of family identity and heavenly pleasure into your heart.

Some of us have heard stories in modern day culture when people have literally glowed with the glory of God. It is my belief in the days to come, as the glory and presence of heaven is released on the earth, this scripture will be fulfilled before our eyes. We have been given a glorious salvation indeed!

Now that we have rebuilt our new birth the "grace way" (remember, we have been saved by grace—this is all by grace), we are going to talk further about the effortless, transforming power that has been given to us "in Christ." What marvelous freedom!

Chapter 9
Transformed by Grace

What we have discussed so far has been things that happen rather suddenly in our spirit, soul, and body when grace touches them. However, one of the biggest criticisms levied against the grace lifestyle is contained in the idea of transformation. Many will agree that when the power of grace is released on us, certain things change. Where the agreement ends is when we start talking about the process of change and growth that happens in each one of us until the day we die. We are all acutely aware of our need for transformation, but when those who adhere to a lifestyle of grace start talking about change happening effortlessly, the gloves come off rather quickly. In order to discover the true transforming power of grace, we are first going to talk about some ways we should not be transformed.

We have already discussed the idea of repentance; one of the main sticking issues. The problem is, *effortless* change seems too good to be true. Most traditional spiritual thinking gives repentance the prime role in transformation. For this reason we are going to give it a little more attention.

Repentance – More than One Kind

I would like to point out that there is a big difference between Old Testament and New Testament repentance. However, in the New Testament, there is also a difference between the repentance of a person coming to Christ for the first time and the repentance we experience under grace. Let us sort out these distinctions. During the time of the Law, repentance was a soul-searching, gut-wrenching ordeal. You will find numerous Old Testament references with the flavor, "Repent, or face dire consequences!" We need only look at Psalm 51 to see what David experienced when he messed up. When we turn the pages of our Bible over to Matthew 3, we see John the Baptist preaching a heavy repentance message complete with colorful threats of hell-fire and brimstone. Keep in mind that this ministry was still under the Law. Jesus had not yet been revealed as the Son of God, and the reconciliation of grace was at least three years away.

When Jesus came on the scene, He also began preaching repentance, but from a different angle. The hard edge of repentance was gone, revealing a new, softer, "grace model" of this gift. The only time when old-school repentance would make an appearance was when He was dealing with ultra-religious people, such as the scribes and Pharisees. It is this New Covenant version of repentance I would like to explore. Let's start with some basic principles of faith. There is a short list of them at the beginning of Hebrews 6:

> *Therefore leaving the elementary teaching about the Christ, let us press on to maturity, not laying again a foundation of repentance from dead works and of faith towards God, of instruction about washings and laying on of hands, and the resurrection of the dead and eternal judgment.* (Hebrews 6:1-2)

First of all, the purpose of this scripture is to point the way to maturity, and the road to maturity always involves growth and change. Second, I want to be clear that I believe in repentance. Not only do I believe in it as a starting place for the Christian life, I also believe it has a place in the ongoing maintenance of the Christian life. Even so, there is much confusion over what it means to repent.

Definitions

A simple definition of the New Testament Greek word for repent, "metanoeo,"

> *A simple definition of the New Testament Greek word for repent, "metanoeo," is to think differently, to reconsider.*

is to think differently, to reconsider. It has elements of revers-
ing a decision, reformation, compunction, and making
change, but the mainstay of this word is the idea of making
a correction in thinking. I would also like to mention that the
words "repent" (metanoeo) and "transform" (metamorphoo)
are closely related in the Greek language. In fact, Strong's
Concordance lists these two words right next to each other
in sequence. They also share the same root word "meta,"
which means to affect a sequence of change. In the case of
"metanoeo," the change is in the realm of thought and direction, whereas in the case of "metamorphoo," it is a change in
character, a transformation, or a transfiguration. Notice how
the writer of Hebrews talks about repentance in the verse
we just quoted. It is referred to as a foundation or a starting
point. To be specific, he is talking about "repentance from
dead works."

We have spent much time discussing the sin-nature,
how the body of flesh is now dead, and how we have been
made into a new being. The dead works referred to are the
ones that were done while we were in the flesh. When we
become born-again, the first thing we do is to repent of these
dead works, resulting in them being removed from us as
far as the east is from the west. In this single action, the sin-
nature and the dead works both go down the eternal drain

together. There is no point in trying to go back and find them: they are gone forever.

Now let us talk for a moment about a person who has not yet been born again by looking at a verse in John 16. Here Jesus is talking about the ministry of the Holy Spirit:

And He, when He comes, will convict the world concerning sin and righteousness and judgment. (John 16:8)

Notice how it says here the Holy Spirit will convict the "world." I would like to remind any born-again person that you are in the world, but not of it (John 17:16), meaning you are free from this conviction. Here is a similar reference spoken by Jesus in the book of Luke:

"It is not those who are well who need a physician, but those who are sick. I have not come to call the righteous but sinners to repentance." (Luke 5:31-32)

This verse contains awesome news for a righteous person. However, for a nonbeliever there is a conviction that needs to come and a repentance that needs to occur in order to gain first-time entrance into the kingdom. Once done, the foundation is laid. There is no purpose served in repeatedly digging it up and trying to re-lay it, as if it were the main tool in our journey towards maturity. Are there times when we need to pull this tool out again? Absolutely! But the way we are told to use it most of the time doesn't make sense, and can be quite destructive.

Where Grace Cannot Reach

I have a bit of trouble with the idea of mandatory sad emotion being associated with "true repentance." I have seen people repent, change their way of thinking, and change their direction in a moment of clarity with absolutely no emotion. However, in all fairness, Paul does reference repentance with sorrow, but he describes it as repentance without regret (2 Corinthians 7:10). If you are experiencing regret in the context of this gift, you are looking at yourself, bowing the knee to law, and receiving death rather than life. I have also seen people supposedly repent with great emotion and duress, only to go back to the same patterns in a matter of days. Let's look at a passage in Hebrews that describes this scenario:

> *See to it that no one comes short of the grace of God; that no root of bitterness springing up causes trouble, and by it many be defiled; that there be no immoral or godless person like Esau, who sold his own birthright for a single meal. For you know that even afterwards, when he desired to inherit the blessing, he was rejected, for he found no place for repentance, though he sought for it with tears.* (Hebrews 12:15-17)

Notice the first thing these verses emphasize is a warning not to fall short of the grace of God. Then the passage mentions two things: first, making sure we don't have bitterness in our lives; and second, making sure we guard our birthright. So what is our birthright? It is simple and glorious: we are joint-heirs with Christ, children of grace. Let's look at Esau. He sold his birthright, then later desired to inherit a blessing (a work of grace). He found no repentance even though he cried many tears, because he had put himself in a position where grace couldn't reach. There is another similar verse of Scripture:

> *You have been severed from Christ, you who are seeking to be justified by law; you have fallen from grace.* (Galatians 5:4)

Again we see a picture of someone who has been severed from Christ and their birthright "in Him." They are trying to justify themselves, or, in other words, find righteousness through the Law. This verse tells us they have fallen from grace. I'm sure Esau had many reasons in his mind justifying why it was a good idea to sell his birthright, but there was no remedy for his situation. If we look at the evil we have done and make a decision to fix things, albeit with many tears, we cannot find the place of repentance because there is no life in this approach to transformation. In our own strength we have no power to make a life-altering change in our lives. What we will be activating is a form of self-discipline rather than the power of God needed for lasting transformation. We are putting our eyes on the wrong thing; we are eating from the wrong tree.

> *I*n our own strength we have no power to make a life-altering change in our lives.

Avoid putting yourself in a position where you have to look at yourself. Stay away from situations where others will tell you to look at yourself. All you will see is your own nakedness. It will make you feel bad. You might cry, you might feel sorry for yourself or for what you have done, you might even recite it out loud, but there will be no repentance in this state. There is only one person in this situation whom we should be looking at: Jesus Christ.

Grace Repentance

Now let us look at what I believe is the true "grace model" for repentance. It is actually an effortless gift of God. I must warn you: this model is going to seem too easy. If you adhere to the traditional notion of this gift, the next few paragraphs could leave you feeling angry or numb. However, if you're looking for something new and life giving, hang on for some excitement.

> *Therefore I urge you, brethren, by the mercies of God, to present your bodies a living and holy sacrifice, acceptable to God, which is your spiritual service of worship.* (Romans 12:1)

Before we talk about this scripture, there is one small detail I want to point out. In some translations, the word "worship" does not appear in this verse. However, in the original text there is one Greek word that encompasses the phrase "service of worship," "latreuo," which means a ministry unto God, a divine act of devotion or worship.

Worship

Paul is talking about presenting our now sin-free bodies as a sacrifice to God. It is important to note that the context of the verse we have just quoted is one of worship. Because of this fact, we are going to talk about worship for a few moments. It is a simple concept that has been around since the beginning of time. In the Old Testament, the first mention of the word "worship" is in the context of Abraham sacrificing Isaac on the mountain in the land of Moriah. The main Hebrew word used for worship both in this text and throughout the Old Testament is "shachah." It means to prostrate in homage to royalty, to bow, or to do reverence. The picture presented in this word is one of coming before a King or Queen, prostrating oneself in front of the Majesty, and paying homage to him or her:

> *Abraham said to his young men, "Stay here with the donkey, and I and the lad will go over there; and we will worship and return to you."* (Genesis 22:5)

Here we find the classic story of Abraham, the sacrifice of Isaac, and the ram caught in the thicket. This pre-law incident is found in Genesis 22:1-19, and I would highly recommend anyone interested in the subject of "worship" to study this text thoroughly. The narrative sets a standard for godly worship as it weaves its way through the Bible. Although there are numerous points to ponder from this account, we will only touch on a few of them briefly. First, worship is always seen in the context of some type of sacrifice. Second, worship needs to be done by faith. Hebrews 12:17-19 tells us Abraham actually believed God would raise Isaac up from the ashes if necessary. Third, it is interesting to note that this occurrence is where God first chose to reveal Himself as "Yahweh Yirah," meaning, "the Lord Will Provide," or "God sees" (Genesis 22:14). Our sacrifices of worship are noted by God and create a window for Him to pour out abundant, timely, and fitting provision on us. Fourth, it was also in this context that God spoke a mind-boggling prophetic word of destiny over Abraham, showing him a snapshot of God's will and purpose for both his life and subsequent generations.

Under the Law, worship was something that, for the most part, revolved around the Tabernacle and Temple. God's people would bring offerings to Him, these items would be sacrificed, and these acts comprised their expression of worship. Most often an animal was sacrificed, but there were other sacrifices as well, such as grain offerings, wave offerings, and first fruits.

Under King David's rule, the existing system of sacrificial worship was augmented with a new dynamic, lasting for a few generations, as a type and foreshadowing of worship under the New Covenant. David ushered in a season when praise, music, singing, and instrumental worship were offered to the Lord around the clock in front of the Ark of the Covenant (1 Chronicles 16:1-4). Under this system, worship became more of a sacrificial offering of the heart and a response to God rather than a sacrifice of animals (Psalm 51:15-17).

"*Proskuneo*," *implies bringing a sacrifice, bowing down, paying homage, and worshipping.*

In the New Testament, worship continues as a priority for God's people and there are two Greek words translated as "worship." The first, "proskuneo," means virtually the same thing as its Hebrew counterpart "shachah." It implies bringing a sacrifice, bowing down, paying homage, and worshipping. Then there is "latreuo," which we have already mentioned. This word implies that our lifestyle and service to the Lord is the act of worship.

> "*Latreuo*" implies that our lifestyle and service to the Lord is the act of worship.

In the first case the sacrifice of worship is more of an event, whereas in the second case it is a 24/7 rendering of our life as a sacrifice.

It is not our goal here to do an in-depth study on this subject, as there are many great books and resources available to those who are interested; however, I would like to point out a few key things. First, worship is still a royal act of sacrifice. Second, the glory of God is always evident during worship. Sometimes in Old Testament accounts, God's presence would manifest as fire falling on the sacrifice, consuming what was on the altar. It is no different today. When we worship, God still sends His glory down on our sacrifice. For this reason, His presence can often be felt in moments of worship. I find if I turn my heart towards God, begin to express my affection for Him, and patiently wait, He is very faithful in this regard. The manifestation of glory might vary in intensity; from my heart simply being warmed, to an all-out encounter, but His presence is always there in some form. Third, we become like whatever we are worshiping.

> *Professing to be wise, they became fools, and exchanged the glory of the incorruptible God for an image in the form of corruptible man and of birds and four-footed animals and crawling creatures. They exchanged the truth of God for a lie, and worshiped and served the creature rather than the Creator, who is blessed forever. Amen.* (Romans 1:22, 23, 25)

What these verses tell us is that there is an exchange that happens in worship. We exchange our glory for the glory of whatever we are worshiping (1 Corinthians 15:38-41, everything created has its own glory). In this Romans narrative, the worshippers exchanged their glory for the glory of a lower form of life, such as a bird or some other animal, because they were worshiping that image. In the end, a further study of this text tells us their bodies became dishonored and they were turned over to lust and impurity because of the transfer. Had the same people been worshiping God, they would have been exchanging the glory which was on them for the glory of God Himself, and they would have become more like Him.

In my estimation, this substitution is a pretty good deal. We offer up our bodies as a living sacrifice and what do we get in exchange? The very glory of heaven rests on us, and we are changed into God's image (and remember, we were originally made in His image and likeness). It is in this context we find the follow-up to the verse we quoted a few paragraphs ago:

> *Therefore I urge you, brethren, by the mercies of God, to present your bodies a living and holy sacrifice, acceptable to God, which is your spiritual service of worship. And do not be conformed to this world, but be transformed by the renewing of your mind, so that you may prove what the will of God is, that which is good and acceptable and perfect.* (Romans 12:1-2)

What I find most interesting is how this transformation (metamorphoo) takes place. The Bible describes it as a "renewing of the mind." Do you remember our definition of repentance a few paragraphs ago? It was a change in thinking, a reversal of a direction of thought. The process of renewing our mind is ongoing in the Christian life, and it is one and the same as the process of repentance. In order to repent, what needs to happen? We need to start thinking differently about where we are and what we are doing, which is having our mind renewed. Jesus would often cry out: "Repent for the kingdom of heaven is at hand" (Matthew 4:17). What exactly was He saying? He was stating that in the kingdom of heaven, everything works opposite to the ways of the earth. For this reason, we need to repent and change our way of thinking, flipping our thought processes upside down, in order to enter His kingdom. Out of this mind-renewal comes transformation, change, and a course correction towards the will of God for our lives.

Now let's consider the process of this transformation in the context of worship. First, we enter the presence of our Father God by faith, bowing before Him, presenting our bodies as a royal act of worship; an act embodying the meaning of the Greek word "proskuneo" (to prostrate in homage to royalty or God, to bow

> *The process of renewing our mind is ongoing in the Christian life, and it is one and the same as the process of repentance.*

down, or to do reverence). Our sacrifice is possible because the old nature in our bodies is dead. However, because our bodies are now holy, acceptable, and alive in Him, we are also able to present our bodies as a "living sacrifice." We are now carrying out an act of service illustrating the meaning of the Greek word "latreuo" (a ministry unto God, a divine act of devotion or worship, or a lifestyle of worship). In this position, there is only one logical place to look: directly at God. As we behold Him, while offering ourselves in worship, we are wrapped up in His grace, His truth, and His love, and our minds become set on Him. His glory then begins to rest on us, and the age-old mystical wonder of the "worship exchange" takes place. In other words, as we focus on Him, we exchange who we are for who He is—all of us for all of Him. We are transformed, our minds are renewed, we begin to think and become like Him, and we begin to understand His will—those things which are good and acceptable and perfect—and the destiny of God is released over us.

Could it Really be that Simple?

In this context we find a true, New Testament, biblical understanding of repentance. True grace repentance is nothing more than being transformed into the image of Jesus while worshipping Him, fixing our eyes on Him, and resting in His

> *In the quest for transformation; repentance, new thought processes, and new directions are discoveries of grace rather than an effort to purge ourselves of sin.*

presence. It is profoundly simple—we first turn away from one thing and then we turn towards another. I might add that we have little to offer to this process apart from the choice of where to focus our eyes. To think otherwise, amounts to nothing but pride. Traditional reasoning is obsessed with the notion of "working with great emotional duress" for repentance, but I am tenderly inviting you to consider the "grace model" of this incredible gift. In the quest for transformation; repentance, new thought processes, and new directions are discoveries of grace rather than an effort to purge ourselves of sin. However, if you find yourself in need of forgiveness, one thing is certain: focusing on the ugliness of sin, and begging for forgiveness in a state of shame, will only reap more sin in your life. On the other hand, if you fix your eyes on Jesus, you only need whisper the request for forgiveness, taking a fraction of a second. Then, spend the rest of the time looking at Him—He is the only one who can transform you into a person who won't do the same thing again. You can't work for repentance; any tears that are shed are those of adoration, the transformation is absolutely effortless.

I stumbled upon this understanding quite by accident some years ago. I grew up in a very strict household, and most of my church experience was quite legalistic. By the time I was in my early teen years, the patterns of repeating the same sins and asking forgiveness for them time and time again were well established in my life. I struggled against certain things for years on end, but to no avail. Being that I had a sensitive nature, I remember few times when I was actually happy because I constantly felt like I was letting God down. Every time there was an altar call at church, and again in my own quiet time, I would bring up my sins, feel sorry for them, and beg God to help me become an overcomer.

As I ventured further in life, these patterns only became worse. The biggest struggle I faced was in my mind, and I often wondered if there was any way to be free. Every time I read or heard a sermon about how God wanted full control over my heart, I felt defective. Eventually I gave up my struggles and yielded to the dark thoughts of my mind, as it seemed much easier. At this point bad patterns became secret addictions. I felt like I was living a lie; a good Christian person on one hand, and a bad defeated sinner on the other. I didn't know at the time, but the very things I was trying to get free from were the things I was focusing on and thinking about. For this reason I lived a life of defeat.

Being a musician, I always had a heart for worship, and about 10 years ago I got a revelation from the Holy Spirit of what it meant to worship in "spirit and in truth" (John 4:23-24). Even through my struggles, I remember clearly taking my guitar into a quiet room, singing, and worshiping for hours, though I had little idea what I was doing. I was desperate to know God, and I worshipped in this manner for what seemed like weeks on end. Every day I would worship, sometimes for one, two, or even three hours straight, depending on how much time I had. A couple of months into my newfound passion, I had a strange experience. I recall waiting on the Lord one afternoon and suddenly thinking, "Hey, I haven't had a particular thought pattern for, wow, at least two or three weeks now." It actually shocked me because these secret, murky contemplations were something I had struggled with before almost daily.

I continued worshiping over the next month or so and realized the thought patterns and subsequent sinful actions were dropping off me effortlessly. After a period of about four months I hardly recognized my own heart. I remember thinking, "You've got to be kidding me. Is this really all there is to it? Why didn't anybody tell me?" I was actually quite upset about it. Here was a lifetime of struggling, supposed "traditional style" repentance, and cyclical destructive patterns wiped out in a few short months in the presence of God. My mind was being renewed: I thought differently, my actions followed suit, addiction was broken, and I became so grateful and in love with Jesus I hardly knew what to do with myself. This occurrence was my first experience with the power of "grace transformation" at work in my life without me even knowing about it.

For this reason it is too late to tell me I have to work for my repentance. From that moment on I have not cried one more tear over sin. If I do something wrong (and we all do from time to time), I simply and quickly take it to God, leave it with Him, and immediately put my eyes back where they belong—on Him!

Two Roads

I have both seen and experienced two roads in regard to repentance. If we insist on having righteousness based on the Law (Galatians 2:21), then we will need to revert back to gut-wrenching law repentance. The only way this lifestyle can be maintained with a clear conscience is through hard work—by self-discipline, sheer will power, flesh defeating practices, and by attaching negative emotional energy to the repentance process. On the other hand, if we believe we have been made fully righteous in Christ, then we (in the words of Jesus - Luke 5:32), have not been called to this kind of repentance. Instead, we have been called to a repented (turned) lifestyle where our minds and hearts

> *We have been called to a repented (turned) lifestyle where our minds and hearts are continually turned towards His face.*

are continually turned towards His face. In this stance, our thinking is constantly renewed to the realities of the kingdom; the transformation is instinctive and joyful rather than gut-wrenching and sorrowful.

I have been in multiple situations through the years where church leaders with an evangelistic bent have leveled the double barreled shotgun of repentance at a group of precious sheep (who have been made righteous in Christ) for weeks on end. The motivations seem to be twofold. First, they are trying to spread a net for unbelievers. Second, they are trying to inspire revival, even though no revival could survive for long in this setting. In the process, sin and death is projected on the flock. I would like to suggest that if preaching sin-repentance were effective, the church would have been sin-free long ago. Instead, the body of Christ is steeped in rampant sin as a result of this mindset—oftentimes the worst offenses being committed by the very people who are doing the preaching. There is good reason why we are in such a mess. As already stated, these practices release the very opposite result to what we are trying to accomplish.

No Longer Naked

I have also seen multiple examples where the presence of the Holy Spirit has come into a room, and immediately the leaders begin to call people to repentance. The assumption is that we need to do "business with God" in this environment. However, the knee-jerk tendency to look at our own naked-ness in the presence of God is a throw-back to the garden. It is a reaction inherited through eating from the wrong tree. In the Old Testament, nakedness was always referred to in the context of shame. The question remains—are we still naked? Friends, we don't need to search very far in the Bible to find numerous references to how we have been clothed in righ-teousness, how we have put on Christ, or how we have been "glorified" and "wrapped up" in Him. As a result, I have a superb newsflash for you: in Christ we are no longer naked—thank you Jesus! We no longer need to look at ourselves in shame when His presence arrives. Resist this temptation. It is a leftover residue from the curse, a byproduct of the fear of breaking law and then being tried, judged, and condemned. In Christ there is no longer any con-demnation. There is only one way to react when Jesus honors us with His presence—keep our eyes locked on Him and Him alone. In this position, there will be intimacy, com-munion, and lasting transformation.

> *There is only one way to react when Jesus honors us with His presence—keep our eyes locked on Him and Him alone.*

True grace repentance is beautiful and effortless. You can try to work for your repentance if you like, but as for me, I receive this gift as a child. I will not insult the blood of Jesus by working up one more drop of sweat to do for myself what He did for me and I will never again dig up and re-lay the foundation of repentance from dead works in my life.

Let's now look at some additional scripture that talks about the renewal of the mind. For this reading I would like to quote the J.B. Phillips translation:

> *What you learned was to fling off the dirty clothes of the old way of living, which were rotted through and through with lust's illusions, and, with yourselves mentally and spiritually remade, to put on the clean fresh clothes of the new life which was made by God's design for righteousness and holiness which is no illusion.* (Ephesians 4:22-24, JBP)

When we renew our mind we put on the new self, created in God's image. What freedom it is to be mentally and spiritually remade. The new birth has recreated us in nature spirit, soul, and body.

Goodness Leads to Repentance

Before we leave the subject of repentance there is another passage in Romans that would be beneficial to look at:

Or do you despise the riches of His goodness, forbearance, and longsuffering, not knowing that the goodness of God leads you to repentance. (Romans 2:4, NKJV)

This scripture is referencing an event back in Exodus, when Moses asked to see the glory of God. The Lord responded by taking Moses to a cleft in the rock and letting all of His "goodness" pass before him (Exodus 33:18-23). The goodness of God is a visible expression of His glory, and according to this verse it is something that brings us to a place of repentance. The most life-altering moments of transformation I have experienced personally have not come from a sin-conscious mindset but an encounter with the goodness of God. Think for a moment about the woman who was caught in the act of adultery and brought before Jesus. The encounter she had with His goodness changed her life, whereas an encounter with the Law would have definitely produced death for her. Jesus literally told her, "I do not accuse you, go and sin no more" (John 8:1-11). When we encounter the goodness and grace of God, there is no other response but to be changed.

Transformed by Glory

With these thoughts in mind, let's take a look at another transformation scripture. This one is found in 2 Corinthians, and it is one of my favorite passages in the Bible. The entire third chapter of this book talks about the Law and how it was given to Moses with glory. It tells us that the glory was so strong Moses had to put a veil over his face when he went to meet with the sons of Israel. However, the main point of this chapter is: if the Law was given with glory, how much greater is the glory of the New Covenant? It then goes on to say the veil is lifted in Christ. In this context we find the following verses:

> But whenever a person turns to the Lord, the veil is taken away. Now the Lord is the Spirit, and where the Spirit of the Lord is, there is liberty. But we all, with unveiled face, beholding as in a mirror the glory of the Lord, are being transformed into the same image from glory to glory, just as from the Lord, the Spirit. (2 Corinthians 3:16-18)

This scripture is packed full of life-altering power. First, it speaks of the freedom of grace that is found when we are spirit-led. Then, in this state, we see a picture of a person looking into a mirror with an unveiled face. Now I have a question for you. Think back to the last time you looked into a mirror. What did you see? Yourself of course! However, what the person in this verse sees is not himself/herself, but the glory of the Lord. A bit atypical, yes, but there is a reason for this anomaly, and it is extremely good news. The Bible says we have died and our lives are now "hidden in Christ"

(Colossians 3:3-4). This person cannot see himself/herself because he/she is quite invisible. What he/she sees instead is Christ in all His glory because he/she is "in Him."

Have you ever heard the statement, "When God looks at you, all He sees is Jesus?" Well, a similar thing is happening here. As we behold the risen Christ in His glory, we are transformed into the same image, from glory to glory—a profound and simple picture of the Greek word "metamorphoo." So what exactly has this person done? He/she has "turned to the Lord," looked at Him with an unveiled face, and yielded to wave after wave of glory! We have talked about this reality before, but let's say it again: it's all about where you put your eyes. It has been that way from the beginning of time! If you want to be

> *As we behold the risen Christ in His glory, we are transformed into the same image, from glory to glory.*

changed, remember that the last person you should be gazing at is yourself. No matter what, it won't be pretty. If you want to look like Jesus, put your eyes on Him, behold His glory, and yield to the effortless transformation.

This transformation model is not something you can work for; it is an empowerment of grace in your life. In this context you will experience freedom you never dreamed possible. You will begin to instinctively live a grace-impregnated, sin-free lifestyle because you are eating from the tree of life instead of trying to figure out how to stay away from doing bad things.

Transformed by the Word

I want to mention one more transforming agent before moving on. In some ways we have already mentioned this means of change, but in a roundabout way. Jesus is referred to in the Bible as the Word. One way we can behold His glory is by looking at this Word. By this statement I mean listening to Him.

Logos

There are at least three different Greek words used for "word" in the New Testament. I will list them briefly and then discuss the implication of each one. The first one is the Greek word "logos." It refers to something "spoken" by God. Here is a scriptural example of this usage:

> *In the beginning was the Word, and the Word was with God, and the Word was God. And the Word became flesh, and dwelt among us, and we saw His glory, glory as of the only begotten from the Father, full of grace and truth.* (John 1:1, 14)

Rhema

The second is the word "rhema." It refers to something "revealed" by God. Here are a couple of scripture verses with this particular meaning:

It is the Spirit who gives life; the flesh profits nothing; the words that I have spoken to you are spirit and are life. (John 6:63)

For nothing will be impossible with God. And Mary said, "Behold, the bondslave of the Lord; may it be done to me according to your word." (Luke 1:37-38)

Graphe

The third Greek word is "graphe." It refers in specific to something "written" by God. This word is often translated "scripture." Here is a New Testament reference for this meaning:

All scripture is inspired by God and profitable for teaching, for reproof, for correction, for training in righteousness; so that the man of God may be adequate, equipped for every good work. (2 Timothy 3:16-17)

Anytime the "word of God" is spoken to us on a basic level, the New Testament refers to it as the "logos" of God.

I would like to point out that even this basic word of God is saturated with the glory of heaven as referenced in John 1:14, and it can include reading scriptures as well as hearing the voice of God in many other ways. As we take this "logos" and meditate on it, we are transformed in the process, and once again it is an effortless change. John describes it as pruning, and Jesus states that we are clean because of the word (logos) He has spoken to us (John 15:1-3). There is a constant auto-course correction to the yielded spirit that is deeply rooted in the word and also a washing effect that we are going to talk about shortly. However, this renewal can be felt in more than just our spirit and soul. There is a passage in Hebrews that sheds some light on another resplendent aspect of the "logos" of God:

> For everyone who partakes only of milk is unskilled in the word of righteousness, for he is a babe. But solid food belongs to those who are of full age, that is, those who by reason of use have their senses exercised to discern both good and evil. (Hebrews 5:13-14 NKJV)

The "word (logos) of righteousness," is something that, according to these verses, can train our "senses" to discern good and evil. The question is: what part of our human makeup do the senses belong to? Our body of flesh! This scripture is saying that the good news of how we have been made righteous in Christ can re-energize and train even our bodies. As a result, our flesh can instinctively and effortlessly recognize and deal with matters of good and evil. We are put in a position not unlike David when he wrote: "My soul thirsts for You, my flesh yearns for You" (Psalm 63:1). Friends, this glorious thought takes us far past the notion that our bodies are still carnal and sin-nature inhabited.

With this point being made, I want to say that the Word, as personified in Jesus, is living, which means He is a person. It is important we do not get ourselves into the position described in John 5:

> *You search the scriptures* [graphe] *because you think that in them you have eternal life; it is these that testify about Me; and you are unwilling to come to Me so that you may have life.* (John 5:39-40)

It is possible to read multiple chapters of the Bible every day and still not know the Word. The Word is more than ink on a page; it is a revelation of Jesus. In this context we find the meaning of the word "rhema." When the "rhema word" of God comes to you, it is by revelation. In fact, once meditated upon and integrated into our human spirit, the "logos" of God can become His "rhema" to us. I would like to suggest that this scenario is highly desirable in our quest for transformation. There is a quote I have heard spoken quite often in

Christian circles and it bears true in this context: "One word from God can change your life forever." Once the "rhema" of God hits you, transformation will either be instant, or in the not-too-distant future. This form of God's word is extremely powerful and life-altering.

Once again, keep your eyes on Jesus, continually "come" to Him as John 5:40 so graciously emphasizes. If you are studying and reading scripture, gently invite the Holy Spirit to help you see Jesus in and through the text. This Holy Spirit partnership is especially important if you are reading places where there is law and command-ment. Always consider the context of the scriptures in relation to the era in which you live; the age of grace.

> *While studying and reading scripture, gently invite the Holy Spirit to help you see Jesus in and through the text.*

Seeing

At this point I would like to touch on the "seeing" realm. As mentioned, the Word may come to us in many ways other than reading the Bible, and the entry place to these realms is communion with Jesus. As we commune with Him, we learn to hear His voice, but hearing is only the starting place. There are many other aspects to this lifestyle I invite you to discover. If our earthly bodies were made to integrate into the physical world, then our human spirits were also created to integrate into the spiritual world. I would like to suggest that each physical sense we have—hearing, taste, touch, smell, sight—are all mirrored in the spirit realm. There is one verse in the Old Testament alone that covers two of these senses: "O **taste** and **see** that the Lord is good" (Psalm 34:8, emphasis mine).

Have you ever thought of the possibility of "seeing" Jesus? Have you ever pondered this verse: "Blessed are the pure in heart, for they shall see God" (Matthew 5:8)? If you talk with someone over the telephone, you will have a significant level of communication; however, if you are face to face with that same person, the amount of perception and intimacy is multiplied infinitely. In my experience, most Christians have settled for a long-distance telephone relationship with Jesus—one in which they leave recorded messages and don't expect a call back. They do not know a face-to-face encounter with Him is not only plausible, but entirely

> *Most Christians have settled for a long-distance telephone relationship with Jesus—one in which they leave recorded messages and don't expect a call back.*

possible and desirable. In this place of intimacy, I find both the "logos" and "graphe" word of God become "rhema" quickly, and life-changing glory is released into me like lightning. Also, an environment of communion, stewarded daily, releases the voice of life in the most unusual times and places. It is constantly being transmitted through life circumstances, inner voices, thoughts, other people (both saved and unsaved), dreams and visions, and other prophetic experiences. The "rhema" or "revealing" of Jesus through the Spirit is always transforming and life-giving. We are never left the same once we encounter Jesus. Before leaving this thought, there is one additional passage of scripture I would like to take a look at. We will read it in two different translations:

> *Beloved, now we are children of God, and it has not appeared as yet what we will be. We know that when He appears, we will be like Him, because we will see Him just as He is.* (1 John 3:2 NASB)

> *Beloved, now we are children of God; and it has not yet been revealed what we shall be, but we know that when He is revealed, we shall be like Him, for we shall see Him as He is.* (1 John 3:2 NKJV)

This verse is talking about the return of Jesus, and how we will be forever changed into His image at His appearing.

What I find intriguing is how this final, glorious transformation takes place. Evidently we are changed when He is revealed and we "see Him" just as He is. I would like to suggest that the process of "metamorphosis" into the image of Jesus has never been any different. One of the foundations of human nature is as follows: we become the likeness of that which we look at. We are all on a course of change, one that will ultimately transform us into His full likeness; however, once again I pose the question: how far do you want to go today?

> *One of the founda-tions of human nature is as follows: we become the likeness of that which we look at.*

I for one, have laid down my life to be a person who hopes and yearns to see Jesus daily, as well as someone who loves the day of His appearing (2 Timothy 4:8). "On earth as it is in heaven" is a fitting declaration for anyone who will put his or her eyes on their Master.

True Holiness

There is another matter that encompasses a high degree of transformational theology—the subject of holiness. There are few concepts that are misconstrued like this one and it is a vast topic; one that could easily fill many volumes.

Consequently, the next few pages will only skim the surface of this incredible gift of God.

Through the years I have been taught that we, as Christians, have trouble staying holy, and that constant self-examination, confession of sin, and repentance is the only way to solve this problem. Consequently, a short while ago I decided to do a study on the subject with no preconceived ideas; just me, my Bible, and the Holy Spirit. I began to systematically look up the numerous New Testament references to holiness, sanctification, cleansing, and purity in varied grammatical tenses. I must admit, the results of my findings took me by surprise.

There are several words in the New Testament translated as holy but the main one is "hagios." It means to be blameless, pure, or set apart. This word speaks of an Old Testament ritual where they would take a vessel intended for use in the sanctuary and sanctify it; cleansing it by a series of sprinklings and washings. It would then be considered holy and set apart for the work of God. There are similar words such as "hagnizo" derived from the same root, translated: to sanctify, to purify, or to cleanse. We will feature scriptures in this section using a number of these words. By far, the majority of the citations I found were directly related to the Holy Spirit. However, I was bemused to find that in the remaining references, not once was the concept of holiness tied together

in context with repentance. In light of this unanticipated discovery, I propose that there might be another dynamic in play
here; another angle from which to view the gift of holiness. I
would like to begin our mini-dissection of this topic with a
series of thought provoking questions.

Previously, we have discussed the fact that the Holy
Spirit could not inhabit the body of a pre-cross human due
to the fact that He could not live in an unholy vessel. We
have also considered how a now born again person, once
again has the Holy Spirit living inside of him/her. My question is: what happens to the Holy Spirit if a Christian sins?
Unquestionably, He cannot exist in an unholy environment,
so what does He do? Does He wince? Does He curl up
in the fetal position inside the person and hide His face in
grief? Does He somehow put up a wall of protection around
Himself (I assume this action might actually protect the
offending person more than the Holy Spirit as sinfulness is
royally torched in His presence)? Does He leave and then
return upon repentance? Or, are we like a house inside, par-
titioned into various rooms—certain ones containing secret
stenches to which He alone has the power to seal the doors?

I do not believe that any of these scenarios contain the
answers to our dilemma. Instead, I would like to suggest that
holiness is a matter of nature. By this I mean: God's very
nature is that He is holy. Arguably, before the cross, there was

no way a person could get rid of the sin-nature that was established at the tree of the knowledge of good and evil. For this reason, the Holy Spirit could not live inside an Old Testament saint. It is also the reason why the road to holiness under the Old Covenant appears quite different than it does today. A study of holiness in the Old Testament reveals a serious, external, law-based procedure, as well as severe consequences in the case of failure.

By contrast, in the new birth, we are profusely blessed by the work of Jesus taking on our old sin-nature into His body on the cross. Because of His sacrifice and blood, we are rid of the sin-nature curse forever. In fact, we

> *We have been made partakers in the divine nature of God rendering us now holy and blameless before Him.*

have now been made partakers in the divine nature of God rendering us holy and blameless before Him—His nature has now become our nature. Here are a few scriptures written in the past tense that illustrate this point:

> *His divine power has granted to us everything pertaining to life and godliness, through the true knowledge of Him who called us by His own glory and excellence. For by*

these He has granted to us His precious and magnificent promises, in order that by them you might become partakers of the divine nature, having escaped the corruption that is in the world by lust. (2 Peter 1:3-4)

Just as He chose us in Him before the foundation of the world, that we should be holy and blameless before Him. (Ephesians 1:4)

Yet He has now reconciled you in His fleshly body through death, in order to present you before Him holy and blameless and beyond reproach—if indeed you continue in the faith firmly established and steadfast, and not moved away from the hope of the gospel that you have heard. (Colossians 1:22-23)

And such were some of you; but you were washed, but you were sanctified, but you were justified in the name of the Lord Jesus Christ, and in the Spirit of our God. (1 Corinthians 6:11)

Cleansing Agents

Now that we have established the source of holiness (the divine nature of God), we are going to delve a bit deeper into the subject. The concept of holiness, without doubt, has a maturing, cleansing, and transforming process attached to it. Holiness is a beautiful gift given to us through the work of the cross. It is then brought to a highly polished finish as a work of grace. It is the very nature of God bestowed upon us and thus, it would be foolish to attempt to work for it. Actually, laboring for it is impossible. Thus, in the following few paragraphs we are going to explore the dynamics of four cleansing agents; one of them dealing with sin, and three of them dealing with holiness, sanctification, and purity.

The Blood of Jesus

The blood of Jesus is a powerful cleansing agent when it comes to sin. In fact, there is no other way to be guiltless apart from His blood. There are numerous scriptures to support this fact but here are a couple of classic verses:

> But if we walk in the light as He Himself is in the light, we have fellowship with one another, and the blood of Jesus, His Son cleanses us from all sin. If we confess our sins, He is faithful and righteous to forgive us our sins and to cleanse us from all unrighteousness. (1 John 1:7, 9)

As mentioned a few pages ago, if you require forgiveness, you need only whisper this confession and request. There is no need to linger here or wallow in shame; doing so will not add one ounce of strength to your struggle against sin. Do it in sincerity, then put your eyes quickly and directly back on Jesus. The sin will be gone permanently and the glory of His face will transform you.

The Water of the Word

A second cleansing agent is the word of God. We will list a couple of scriptures and then discuss their relevance in light of our subject.

> *Husbands, love your wives, just as Christ also loved the church and gave Himself up for her; that He might sanctify her, having cleansed her by the washing of water with the word, that He might present to Himself the church in all her glory, having no spot or wrinkle or any such thing; but that she should be holy and blameless.* (Ephesians 5:25-27)

> *You are already clean because of the word which I have spoken to you.* (John 15:3)

Notice, in these verses we now see a reference to holiness. Keep in mind that there are a couple of different concepts we are dealing with here. The first one is sin and as we have already seen, it is dealt with and cleansed by the blood of Jesus. The second one is the idea of sanctification, purity, and holiness. These two concepts are not one and the same. Holiness is the very nature of God bestowed upon us and these verses cite a different cleansing agent—the water of the word released to perfect holiness in us. Keep in mind that this word is the "logos" word of God.

Let me create a scenario for you. Imagine for a moment that you ended up somewhere and by default were exposed to something sinful—something you just didn't want to see. As a result, you feel slimed, dirty, and possibly violated by evil. You might even feel like you have sinned although you never intended to be put in the position you found yourself in. A first reaction might be to try and repent, which you attempt to do, but to no avail. There is no relief. The reason is: you have been made unclean, but you have not sinned. In other words, the devil has thrown mud on you, it has stuck, and you have been defiled. It is affecting your mind, your very nature, and your ability to proceed with life, and you need to get it off. In these situations, there is only one thing to do—go directly to the word of God (and by this I mean Jesus), and let Him speak to you. The word of God will wash you clean. It is a marvelous cleansing agent. In fact, a life rooted in the abiding word, will keep you so hosed off, you might barely even notice the defilement of the flesh and the stains of the world as they assault you on a daily basis. The result is renewed holiness, purity, and blamelessness and according to the above scripture passages, it is the way Jesus is planning to perfect His bride.

In this context I would like to point out that there were two substances released from the side of Jesus on the day He was crucified:

But one of the soldiers pierced His side with a spear, and immediately there came out blood and water. (John 19:34)

These two elements—the blood and the water are vital for transformation and critical to maintaining our Christian life. They were also mentioned hundreds of years before Jesus by the prophet Zechariah.

In that day a fountain will be opened for the house of David and for the inhabitants of Jerusalem, for sin and for impurity. (Zechariah 13:1)

The fountain that came from Jesus' side took care of sin through His blood, and it also made provision for us to be pure, holy, and blameless before Him through the water of the word—simply phenomenal!

The Fear of the Lord

Here is another holiness perfecting agent. Paul is talking in context about the danger of being bound together with unrighteousness and he makes this statement:

Therefore, having these promises, beloved, let us cleanse ourselves from all defilement of flesh and spirit, perfecting holiness in the fear of God. (1 Corinthians 7:1)

I have a simple and clear question to ask about this verse. Do we have the ability to clean our flesh and our spirit of defilement? I would venture to say that apart from the work of grace in our hearts, we do not even have this ability. We will be relying on will power which will lead us down roads that will invariably reap more sin in our lives. For this reason, rather than trying to embark on a repenting and self-cleansing spree, I would like to suggest that the pathway leading to the holiness spoken of here lies in the phrase, "perfecting holiness in the fear of God." A clear encounter with the reverential fear of God is a powerful cleansing agent. The above verse states that in the context of this revelation, holiness is perfected in us. The Greek word for "perfect" speaks of a process of maturity. Thus, our holiness is made complete or mature as we revel in the environment of the fear of God—a most awesome place to be. Scary, yes! But, awesome all at the same time!

A Revelation of Eternity

Here is another holiness catalyst and it is found in the follow-up verse to the passage in John that we quoted just a few paragraphs ago:

Beloved, now we are children of God, and it has not appeared as yet what we will be. We know that when He appears, we will be like Him, because we will see Him just as He is. And everyone who has this hope fixed on Him purifies himself, just as He is pure. (1 John 3:2-3)

There is a marvelous secret to effortless transformation hidden in this verse. As we fix our hope on His revealing, His appearing, or in other words, in seeing Jesus, it releases a purification process in us. I would like to call this holiness agent a revelation of eternity. It is the realization that there is more to life than what we can see—there is an eternal element. How remarkable is this grace that has been poured out on us; as we fix our hope on eternity and the revealing of the pure Jesus, we are transformed into the same pure image!

To close this subject, here is an inspiring passage that ties the ideas of the fear of the Lord, His revealing, holiness, and grace all together in the same place:

*Therefore, gird your minds for action, keep sober in spirit, fix your hope completely on the **grace** to be brought to you at **the revelation of Christ**. As obedient children, do not be conformed to the former lusts which were yours in igno-rance, but like the Holy One who called you, be **holy** your-selves also in all your behavior; because it is written, "you shall be holy, for I am holy." And if you address as Father* *the One who impartially judges according to each man's work, **conduct yourselves in fear** during the time of your stay upon the earth.* (1 Peter 1:13-17, emphasis mine)

Nobody will argue that the process of growing into maturity is a lifelong journey. We are told to grow up in all aspects in Him (Ephesians 4:15); however, it is futile to try to muster up a growth spurt. Growing up happens naturally in a healthy environment, and maturity comes the same way with time and patience. Never get down on yourself when you see shortcomings or things that don't quite measure up to your ideals. Fix your eyes on Jesus: He alone is able to complete the good work that He started in you, and He has provided a most amazing empowerment of grace to get the job done. Rest, trust, abide, and yield to this divine favor, and the process will be filled with joy rather than sorrow and striving.

In the upcoming pages we are going to explore the new law of love and how it relates to the era of grace into which we have been released.

Chapter 10
The New Law

A bit earlier we talked about how Jesus was able to break the Law down into a few simple phrases, the most well-known of these being the golden rule, "In everything, treat people the same way you want them to treat you, for this is the Law and the prophets" (Matthew 7:12). We also talked about the law of love, or the new commandment if you like. Somehow Jesus knew that love supersedes law and the knowledge of good and evil.

Let's start by making a rather bold statement. In the epoch of grace we now enjoy, we are through with trying to keep law. This new paradigm doesn't mean we live a life devoid of morals; it means that the

> *The empowering agent to live a sin-free lifestyle no longer comes from the Law—it now flows out of grace.*

empowering agent to live a sin-free lifestyle no longer comes from the Law—it now flows out of grace.

> *For sin shall not be master over you, for you are not under law but under grace.* (Romans 6:14)

Notice how the new lifestyle of grace sets us free to live a life without sin. There are numerous scriptures one could look at in support of this fact. But now, let's look at the new commandment of love. If you will recall, Jesus gave us this commandment in John, but then set the standard of love so high it is humanly impossible to reach. In essence, He stated that we should love our neighbors in the same way the Father loved Him. Since God is the personification of love, we are left with a commandment so far beyond our earthly ability, it is almost ridiculous. Once again we see the standard of grace set higher than law. I would like to explore the freedom even in this new law.

I have listened to many sermons and read many books and articles on this subject. Many of them focus on how we are not living up to this standard. At the end of the dissertation, a challenge is given and people are given the chance to make amends in this area of life, to make a decision to love more like Christ. Since Christ loves with perfect love, once again we are put in a position where we are trying to measure up.

We try to be extra kind to our neighbors for a few days, but eventually we run out of steam and slip back into our old patterns and for good reason: we are trying to fulfill law. Any law, no matter how good and noble, is still a

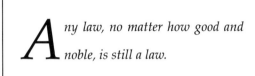

A ny law, no matter how good and noble, is still a law.

law. Before we go any further, let's look at scripture pertaining to this new commandment, which is found throughout the Bible, and has its origins in the Mosaic Law.

You shall love the Lord your God with all your heart and with all your soul and with all your might. (Deuteronomy 6:5)

You shall not take vengeance, nor bear any grudge against the sons of your people, but you shall love your neighbor as yourself; I am the Lord. (Leviticus 19:18)

And He said to him, "You shall love the Lord your God with all your heart, and with all your soul, and with all your mind. This is the great and foremost commandment. The second is like it, you shall love your neighbor as yourself. On these two commandments depend the whole Law and the Prophets." (Matthew 22:37-40)

A new commandment I give to you, that you love one another, even as I have loved you, that you also love one another. (John 13:34)

This is My commandment, that you love one another, just as I have loved you. (John 15:12)

This I command you, that you love one another. (John 15:17)

For the whole Law is fulfilled in one word, in the statement, "You shall love your neighbor as yourself." (Galatians 5:14)

If, however, you are fulfilling the royal law according to the scripture, "You shall love your neighbor as yourself," you are doing well. (James 2:8)

This is His commandment, that we believe in the name of His Son Jesus Christ, and love one another, just as He commanded us. (1 John 3:23)

And this commandment we have from Him, that the one who loves God should love his brother also. (1 John 4:21)

Now I ask you, not as though I were writing to you a new commandment, but the one which we have had from the beginning, that we love one another. And this is love, that we walk according to His commandments. This is the commandment, just as you have heard from the beginning, that you should walk in it. (2 John 1:5-6)

Here we have an impressive list of scriptures with one common purpose: to show us the way to a new commandment. However, let's make one point clear: if we are trying to muster up the ability to keep this commandment, we are serving in the "oldness of the letter" and not in the "newness of the spirit." Thankfully there is an answer to this dilemma, and it is going to seem too easy.

Let us go back and review in brief the passage in Jeremiah talking about the New Covenant and how someday the Law would be written in our hearts:

"But this is the covenant which I will make with the house of Israel after those days," declares the Lord, "I will put My Law within them and on their heart I will write it; and I will be their God, and they shall be my people." (Jeremiah 31:33)

There is another scripture referencing this reform:

And I will give them one heart, and put a new spirit within them. And I will take the heart of stone out of their flesh and give them a heart of flesh. (Ezekiel 11:19)

The New Law of the New Covenant

In my estimation, the new "law of love" is that which is now inscribed inside of us. It is unquestionably the law of the "Spirit of life" in Christ Jesus, as referenced in Romans 8, setting us free from the law of "sin and death." It is the new law of the New Covenant, just as the Mosaic writings were the Law of the Old Covenant, and it is written with the blood of Jesus on the tablets of our hearts.

This new law of love was given a few days before the ushering in of a new era of grace, mere hours before Jesus went to the cross. It was even called a "new commandment." Remember that commandment and law are one and the same. This new commandment supersedes and fulfills all the old law in one simple statement and it has been written with ink that is invisible; out of sight and out of mind. Because we can no longer look at it with our earthly

> *The new "law of love" is that which is now inscribed inside of us.*

eyes, we are empowered to keep the law of love by focusing our eyes on Jesus (the source of life) rather than the old law (the medium of sin and death). The new law of love is the law of grace.

Made Perfect

There is one thing I have noticed in relation to New Testament scriptures that talk about love and the law. It is the idea of being made "perfect"—a concept that we touched on briefly in the previous chapter. Let us read through a few of them to see if we can discover some keys to living this life-style of love. However, before we go on, let us take a quick look at the word rendered in the New Testament as "perfect." It is the Greek word "teleios" and it means to be complete, of full age, and consummate in character. Its Greek roots have overtones of consecration, meaning to be set apart or holy. This word speaks of full maturity of character and of being complete.

Now, here are the verses. I have added some notes before a few of them to give you a bit of the context in which they are set, to avoid quoting lengthy passages, but I encourage you to look them up when time permits.

[Here Jesus is talking about loving our neighbor. He states that our standard of love has to be higher than the tax collectors who love only those who love them back.] *Therefore, you are to be **perfect**, as your heavenly Father is **perfect**.* (Matthew 5:48, emphasis mine)

[Here Paul gives an exhortation on the life of love, commonly known as the "love chapter." He ends by saying that certain things will be done away with but love will always remain.] *But when the **perfect** comes, the partial will be done away.* (1 Corinthians 13:10, emphasis mine)

[Here the writer is talking about the old Law and how it is has been replaced with a better one—the new law of love.] *For, on the one hand, there is a setting aside of a former commandment because of its weakness and the uselessness (for the Law made nothing **perfect**), and on the other hand there is a bringing in of a better hope, through which we draw near to God.* (Hebrews 7:18-19, emphasis mine)

[Here James is referencing the royal law of love, which he speaks about a few verses later.] *But one who looks intently at the **perfect** law, the law of liberty, and abides by it, not having become a forgetful hearer but an effectual doer, this man will be blessed in what he does.* (James 1:25, emphasis mine)

[Here John is talking about the new commandment.]
*But whoever keeps His word, in him the love of God has truly been **perfected**.* (1 John 2:5, emphasis mine)

*No one has seen God at any time; if we love one another, God abides in us, and His love is **perfected** in us.* (1 John 4:12, emphasis mine)

*We have come to know and have believed the love which God has for us. God is love, and the one who abides in love abides in God, and God abides in him. By this, love is **perfected** with us, so that we may have confidence in the day of judgment; because as He is, so also are we in this world. There is no fear in love; but **perfect** love casts out fear, because fear involves punishment, and the one who fears is not **perfected** in love. We love, because He first loved us.* (1 John 4:16-19, emphasis mine)

This selection of verses starts with an impossible statement. It reminds me of Jesus' commandment to love in the same manner as the Father loves. We are told to be perfect even as our heavenly Father is perfect. Then we see that the old Law could not make anybody perfect, but when the new one comes, the old will be done away with; leaving us in a position where we can once again be perfected in love. James describes the law of love as the "perfect law of liberty." This delineation is incredible to ponder: a law that sets us free. Most laws are meant to enforce restrictions, to make people think twice about doing evil, but this one brings freedom. There is only one way to be free from law and that is to have it written inside of you.

Abiding in Love

I believe John was given revelation into this new life-style like no other. The letter he writes is most telling when it comes to how love works. He talks about such things as God abiding in us and then us abiding in His love. If we have welcomed the God who "is love" into our heart, then love abides in us. John tells us that because of this love living in us, we are perfected in love. In other words, we are made fully mature and complete in love, which, in turn, drives fear out of our lives. There is a well-founded reason for the absence of fear in the presence of love.

> *If we have welcomed the God Who "is love" into our heart, then love abides in us.*

If you break a law, what is the first thing that comes to mind? The punishment that will come if someone finds out! Under the old system, trepidation over the consequence of a wrong is exactly what would happen. The morality of the human race was, and still is, more or less checked by the fear of punishment. In a secular, godless society these edicts are a must, however, this succession was never the original intent. It is what happened when we chose a life governed by the knowledge of good and evil rather than a relationship with a heavenly Father who is the essence of love. But we don't have to live this way:

> *For the Law brings about wrath, but where there is no law, there also is no violation.* (Romans 4:15)

Under the new system of grace, there is no more law to break. We have been made perfect due to the fact that Love now abides in us. If we gaze intently, as James suggests, at the "perfect law of liberty," what are we actually doing? Once again, we are fixing our eyes on Jesus. The new law of freedom is the tree of life. If you look at the cross, what do you see? Love personified. Jesus is the perfect law of liberty. This freedom lifestyle is more than trying to keep a new law; it is getting to know love Himself, and it is the reason why John keeps stressing that we abide in love. He repeatedly gives this counsel and then completes the cycle by telling us that love also abides in us. The word abide means "to live or dwell," so we need to literally take up residence in the presence of Love.

So the question remains: if we have been set free from law, is there still a moral code in place for humankind? The answer is yes! Should we be specific about this moral code as laid out in the Bible; making it clearly known down through family lines and teaching it to those under our influence and care? Absolutely! However, if we try to keep this moral code on our own, we will fail. Thankfully, in Christ, a way has been made available for us to instinctively fulfill moral code through living out the new law of love. It is the original lifestyle of abiding we were offered in the beginning; at the creation of our species. Although we rejected our freedom, this love-lifestyle has been re-gifted to us through grace. Think about the Garden of Eden. Adam and Eve lived in the presence of love and in this environment there is no record of them having a moral code. But to them, love was not just a concept, it was a person and that person was none other than their heavenly Father, the God of creation Himself. In the new birth we have once again been connected to this love. In fact *He* lives, abides, dwells, or if you like, has taken up residence within us. Now all that is left for us to do is to effortlessly yield to this love.

Put your eyes on Him; don't take them off. As you gaze at love/Love, you will become like the very thing/Person you are looking at. My friends, there is no other way; it is all about where you look.

There are only two choices. Either we try to justify ourselves, and then feel naked when we miss the mark and don't measure up (this is the literal meaning of the Hebrew word for "sin"—to miss the mark); or we gaze intently in the right direction, and eat from the tree of life. In the latter case, we will find ourselves instinctively living a standard of love far above what we could have imagined possible.

Because He First Loved Us

There is a final part to this equation, and it is found in the last verse we quoted, "We love because He first loved us." I suggest that most of us are trying to love out of a heart that is empty, which is why we tire so quickly in our love walk. We know in theory

> *Most of us are trying to love out of a heart that is empty, which is why we tire so quickly in our love walk.*

that God loves us, but it is theological terminology to us; confined to our heads, and not intuited in our hearts. We have knowledge of this love, but we have never encountered it for ourselves. Have you ever considered the gravity of these statements recorded by John? Here Jesus is talking about His relationship with the Father, His disciples, and all of those who would believe in Him down through the ages:

> *I in them and You in Me, that they may be perfected in unity, so that the world may know that You sent Me, and loved them, even as You have loved Me. And I have made Your name known to them, and will make it known, so that the love with which You loved Me may be in them, and I in them.* (John 17:23, 26)

Notice the use of our word "perfected" here. The love that the Father has for you is the same love that He has for Jesus. I will say it again; God loves you with the same unfathomable intensity with which He loves Jesus. It is one and the same love. Pause and think about that for a moment. It is a stunning revelation. Here is another exceptional scripture in the context of the love of God:

> *So that Christ may dwell in your hearts through faith; and that you, being rooted and grounded in love, may be able to comprehend with all the saints what is the breadth and length and height and depth, and to **know** the love of Christ which surpasses **knowledge**, that you may be filled up to all the fullness of God.* (Ephesians 3:17-19, emphasis mine)

Notice how we are to "know" a love that surpasses "knowledge." This first "knowing" is a deep, experiential, "rhema" type of love encounter; exceeding the ability of our human intellect to comprehend. It is the Greek counterpart to the Hebrew word "yada," found in such Old Testament scriptures as: "now Adam knew Eve his wife" (Genesis 4:1). This love cannot be measured in earthly terms; it can only be given through intimate revelation. I am inviting you on a quest to encounter this love. You see, we can only truly love when we allow ourselves to first be loved by Him; hence the statement, "We love because He first loved us."

Encountered by Love

Hardly a day passes when I don't ask the Holy Spirit to reveal the love of the Father to me. I will sit quietly for minutes, sometimes hours, and let Him love me. Sometimes I will crawl up on His lap, be still, and let the love of heaven embrace me. I frequently ask the Holy Spirit to reveal to me the breadth and length and height and depth of this love, which surpasses knowledge and fills me up with all the fullness of my Father God. Many times these practices result in an incredible, tangible release of the Father's love and presence over me. These moments leave me completely undone. However, I have to be honest, other times there are no "fireworks" and, especially in down times, I come to this source of love solely as an act of faith. Thankfully, even the simplest expression of faith pleases God, and I find that through years of persistence, an incredible, unshakable confidence has built up in my heart when it comes to God's love for me.

In this state we become rooted and grounded in love, and we can love because He has first loved us. In other words, His love is revealed to our hearts first, and only then that same love can be released through us to the world. We can only pour something out of a cup that has something in it. When our hearts lack this divine love encounter, we have nothing to give.

I find in my own life my "love well" dries up pretty quickly if I am not drinking frequently from the source of living water. The reason is: this type of love is a heavenly commodity; we can't get it anywhere else, and if we try to manufacture it on our own, we burn out sooner rather than later. Everything we do and all that we are needs to flow

A "love encountered" life-style, simply put, is the way of the New Covenant.

from intimate, personal experience with this love. A "love encountered" lifestyle, simply put, is the way of the New Covenant.

I encourage you to take the time for this encounter. There is no shortcut. I also exhort you never to let yourself be put in a situation where you are left feeling bad about not living up to a set standard of love, regardless of who has set it. There is only one way to live the lifestyle of grace: effortless transformation. With that statement I set you totally free from trying to keep the commandment of love. Instead, put your eyes on the One you want to be like; Love Himself. Let patience have its "perfect" work, and you will be changed into the same image.

In the next chapter we are going to explore the new birth overflow of bearing fruit by grace, out of this incredible source of love.

Chapter 11
Bearing Fruit by the Spirit

There is one major difference between a lifestyle of grace and law. Under the system of law, we must work for whatever we get as a benefit. By this I mean that any advancements or achievements in our lives are the direct result of hard work, struggle, and the exertion of energy. This notion is imbedded in our culture and our worldview like few other concepts.

For the past 10 years I have been driving by a high school every day on the way to work. There is a large electronic sign out front that scrolls different announcements, school dates, and slogans. One statement that seems to come up repeatedly on this marquee is, "Nothing good comes without effort." I am not trying to say that students should not put effort into their studies, but I am making the point that our world is obsessed with the idea that we must labor intensively for everything we get in life. This training starts at an early age, is perpetuated down through family lines

and businesses, and is often touted as an exceptional personality trait. I can't tell you the number of times I have asked
someone how they are doing, to be answered proudly by
adjectives such as: "I'm swamped," "I'm so busy," or "I'm
exhausted!" For this reason, when it comes to spiritual things,
we default to the belief that the same must be true.

> *E*very person born
> has a calling on
> his or her life.

Even in the natural world,
however, let us remember one
thing; labor and eating our
bread (another way of saying
"making a living") by the sweat
of our brow was introduced as
part of the curse. Before Adam
and Eve sinned, life was much different on this planet. They
still had work to do, but it was not a grievous labor for them.
In fact it was a joy, each day bringing new, untold adven-
ture and fulfillment into their lives. Every person born has a
calling on his or her life. This calling is made up of a combination of unique skills, dispositions, interests, and anointings.
It was God's original intention for these things to seamlessly
translate into the destiny that is on each individual, and ultimately our life's vocation.

Studies have shown that precious few ever reach this
place in life, one when their choice of career mirrors what
they were created to do. Instead we work hard, laboring

by the sweat of our brow, to try and beat the curse that this fallen world has been placed under. Some of us make it higher up the ladder than others, but the Bible is clear that there is "sorrow" attached to anything gained by this system (Proverbs 10:22). Because we are so transfixed on overcoming the obstacle of the curse, people literally mock if you dare suggest an alternate way might be available to them through the cross.

The grace lifestyle has a much different system of gain attached to it. Rather than working hard for everything we get, it is all about bearing fruit. When is the last time you have driven by an orchard and seen the fruit trees striving, busting at the seams with heavy labour, trying to bear fruit? No, instead what you will likely see is a gentle grove of trees stretching their green leaves towards the sun, with roots reaching down into the ground where you can't see them, lapping up water and soil nutrients. Then, if you happen to be driving by in the correct season you will see something else: fruit appearing on the branches. You see, you can't work to bear fruit. It is the natural,

> *You can't work to bear fruit. It is the natural, due process of a healthy and well cared for tree.*

due process of a healthy and well cared for tree. We are going to look briefly at this process as it pertains to our freedom and grace. Let us start with some well-known scripture, some of which we have recently quoted.

> *For you were called to freedom, brethren; only do not turn your freedom into an opportunity for the flesh, but through love serve one another. For the whole Law is fulfilled in one word, in the statement, "you shall love your neighbor as yourself." But I say, walk by the spirit, and you will not carry out the desire of the flesh. But if you are led by the spirit, you are not under the Law.* (Galatians 5:13-14, 16, 18)

Notice what is at stake here: freedom. The lifestyle of grace has made us so free that there are hardly words to describe it. We have a new and invisible law of love written on the inside of our hearts. We have been given tools for transformation and the renewing of our mind that require nothing more of us than to fix our gaze on our Savior and behold His glory. We have been released into doing good things instinctively rather than striving. Here we see the Apostle Paul admonishing us to be responsible with our freedom and to use it as an opportunity for love. He is also very emphatic in saying that if we walk by the spirit, we will not be living out bad things—carrying out the lifestyle of the flesh or the old sinful nature.

Romans 8:9 states that we are in the spirit if Christ is in us. We need not fear oscillating between the spirit and the flesh if we are in Christ. This cerebral vacillation uses up physical, mental, and spiritual energy in an effort to try to stay on the "spirit" side, taking us down the road to law, which leads to sin, which leads to death. No, instead we are fully in Christ and we are quite safe there. In this condition we are released from the Law. We are no longer ruled by our old sin-nature-ridden body because it is dead and buried with Christ. Instead, we are now being guided by our spirit, which is intertwined with the Spirit of God Himself, producing in us life. Remember that grace and law are opposites, so if we are not under law we are indeed under grace (Romans 6:14). It is in this context we find the next part of the Galatians text we are studying.

Works of the Flesh

Now the works of the flesh are evident, which are: adultery, fornication, uncleanness, lewdness, [We have skipped a few choice "flesh works" here for sake of time]... *envy, murders, drunkenness, revelries, and the like; of which I tell you beforehand, just as I also told you in time past, that those who practice such things will not inherit the kingdom of God.* (Galatians 5:19, 21, NKJV)

These deeds are of the old nature, and notice how they are referenced—they are called "works." You see, if you are under the Law you are going to be working for things, and

> *L aw always exacts effort from its adherents.*

here we have a very comprehensive list. It is always that way when you are "trying" to keep commandments and live by the knowledge of good and evil. You will also work for every other thing that proceeds from your life no matter how good, bad, or indifferent. Law always exacts effort from its adherents. Now, let us contrast the next few verses in this narrative.

Fruit of the Spirit

> *But the fruit of the spirit is love, joy, peace, longsuffering, kindness, goodness, faithfulness, gentleness, self-control. Against such there is no law. And those who are Christ's have crucified the flesh with its passions and desires.* (Galatians 5:22-24, NKJV)

Here we find the deeds of the spirit. Notice how they are referenced: they are no longer called "works" but "fruit." These virtues are to be the natural outflow of the spirit-led life, and it is interesting that in this place of rest there is no law. And so, law produces works whereas grace yields fruit. Notice also the depiction of those who are Christ's: we have crucified the flesh, past tense, end of story! The problem is I can't tell you how many times in my life I have tried to work up these fruits. We as humans are infinitely obsessed with this ethic, but let me tell you, grace is an all or nothing lifestyle; there is no middle ground. How many times have I, or others like me, stood up like a Christian aerobics instructor and told people to, "Work it baby!" Then there is the exhortation to take a lesson out of James when he states that faith without works is dead (James 2:17). I would like

> *G* *race is an all or nothing lifestyle; there is no middle ground.*

to follow up this statement with one made by Paul. In many of his writings, Paul uses the illustration of circumcision as the ultimate work of the Law (ouch)! Here are a couple of verses in this context.

> *It was for freedom that Christ set us free; therefore keep standing firm and do not be subject again to a yoke of slavery. For in Christ Jesus neither circumcision nor uncircumcision means anything, but faith working through love.* (Galatians 5:1, 6)

Faith without works might be dead, but the work that faith does is through love, and love is the invisible new law written in our hearts. So, we can try to work all we like, but a better idea might be to rest our eyes on the Lord of Love and let our faith bear fruit the natural "love way." Let me give you a grace-illustrated picture of this type of fruit bearing, found in the words of Jesus:

> *I am the true vine, and My Father is the vinedresser. Every branch in Me that does not bear fruit, He takes away; and every branch that bears fruit, He prunes it so that it may bear more fruit. You are already clean because of the word which I have spoken to you. Abide in Me, and I in you. As the branch cannot bear fruit of itself unless it abides in the vine, so neither can you unless you abide in Me. I am the vine, you are the branches; he who abides in Me and I in him, he bears much fruit, for apart from Me you can do nothing.* (John 15:1-5)

Once again we see the usage of New Covenant language here; this whole passage is talking about abiding. It is up to us as a branch to abide in the vine, or, in other words, take up residence in the presence of Jesus as He has taken up residence in us. The writer is very clear here, quoting Jesus as saying we cannot bear fruit ourselves. In fact, He goes so far as to say, "Without Me you can do nothing!" This bold statement should pretty much convince anybody trying to bear fruit in their own strength that it is futile to work for your fruit. It is infinitely more beneficial to yield to grace rather than attempt to keep law.

Pruning can be Fun

I have heard my share of grizzly exhortations on pruning, but I would like to point out that Jesus releases the listener from the fear of pruning almost immediately after He speaks about it. It is a work of grace in our lives that takes place when we abide in the Word. Once again, the Word is not letters on a page, but Jesus Himself. Pruning is a constant and subtle auto-correction that takes place in an abiding heart, and it is part of the process of effortless transformation and mind-renewal.

Take Your Pick

So, fruit bearing is all about abiding and where we put our eyes. Living in the presence of Love is the grace way. As we abide in this Love, we are rooted and grounded, and we bear fruit the natural way. But there is one more fun fact about fruit that not too many people think about: fruit is meant to be eaten! As we go about our daily lives, with roots deep in the life-giving source, we will inevitably come across situations where people are in need. On these occasions, all we have to do is let them pick from our tree. Maybe there is someone who is having a bad day. Well, let them pick the goodness of the Lord from your tree. Perhaps you will run across someone who has been treated harshly. Let them pick kindness from your tree. If your path intersects with a situation that is devoid of peace, let the people involved feed on the peace that is on you. Don't try to conjure up something that is not there, simply abide in the vine. In this state you are not trying to keep law, you are merely being a tree, rooted and grounded in love, branches stretched up towards heaven, receiving the water of the Word Himself as your source. There is another verse we can look at in regard to bearing fruit and it is found in Colossians.

> [Paul is praying over the Colossian church.] *So that you will walk in a manner worthy of the Lord, to please Him in all respects, bearing fruit in every good work and increasing in the knowledge of God.* (Colossians 1:10)

Notice that in this verse, we are to bear fruit in our works. Once again we see the standard of grace set higher than the standard called for by law. Under the Law we are required to do good works, and if we do this, we do well. Under grace we need to bear fruit in our doing of good works. Merely doing something

> *A fun fact: fruit is meant to be eaten!*

good is not good enough anymore; now it has to be done in conjunction with fruit bearing. For instance, under law you could easily do the good work of giving someone a cup of cold water if they were thirsty. Under grace this same cup of water needs to be given from under the umbrella of the fruit of the spirit; lovingly, patiently, graciously, and with the life-giving compassion of heaven behind it. In one case you will be quenching thirst, in the other you will be ministering life.

From this illustration, we can see why is why it is imperative that we don't try to do "works" on our own strength. In fact, in the words of Jesus, we are incapable (John 15:5). Never let anybody tell you that you should be working harder, longer, or with more fervor for the kingdom. This type of activity leads to nothing but death and burnout, and it is the by-product of our obsession with good and evil; we are trying to justify ourselves by doing good things. Let the rhythms of grace and the fruit of the spirit flow naturally and instinctively out of your life. They will produce works more beautiful and eternal than you ever dreamed possible. Once again, I set you free from trying to bear fruit and do good works. Healthy trees effortlessly bear fruit in season; they don't try. Here is one final Old Testament picture of a fruit-bearer:

How blessed is the man who does not walk in the council of the wicked, nor stand in the path of sinners, nor sit in the seat of scoffers! But his delight is in the law of the Lord, and in His law he meditates day and night. He will be like a tree firmly planted by streams of water, which yields its fruit in its season and its leaf does not wither; and in whatever he does, he prospers. (Psalm 1:1-3)

When reading Scripture we need to be careful that we render it from the grace-side of the cross. For a person with a sensitive heart, it would be easy to look at this passage and start self-examining whether or not we are standing in the path of sinners or sitting in the seat of scoffers. The reason I say this is because I default to this way of thinking myself. We could start a diary, recording the number of hours we clock in meditation on the law of the Lord because these verses tell us we should meditate day and night. Subsequently we could come to the logical conclusion that there is a formula: time put in equals amount of fruit yielded. We could also decide to try and keep the law we are meditating on in order to bear any fruit at all. All of this thinking can lead down a slippery slope pretty quickly. So, let us look at this passage from a grace standpoint. The following rendering is my own paraphrase, to get the point across.

A Gracious Translation

We are the blessed ones who have been released from the council of the wicked and the seat of the scoffers; thank God for His mercy toward us. Always believe the very best of yourself, refuse to think about yourself in any way other than the way God thinks of you. Trust me; He sees the very best in you all the time because He sees you "in Christ." If you look at yourself, you will rarely allow yourself to see anything good. Now, what is the law that we should be meditating on? The law of the New Covenant is Love Himself, so what we should be doing is meditating and fixing our eyes on Jesus in all His glory; referred to in John as "abiding in Him." We have taken up residence in this place of rest and He has come to live with us, implying an effortless 24/7 relationship with Him (i.e., day and night). If we meditate on the word of God, and by this I mean the Bible, we should be doing it with a view to encountering the Living Word rather than reading the dead letter of the Law. In this grace stance, we are put in a position where we can effortlessly bear the fruit talked about in these verses, and our tree will be so well watered that our leaves will never dry up. Also, we will prosper in all we say and do. Glorious!

Everything we are and do needs to flow out of abiding in the vine, taking up residence in the presence, worship, being still in the glory, and gazing upon Love personified.

Hidden in this "Eden" lifestyle, we find the freedom of being led by the spirit and the pathways of grace.

In the upcoming pages we will return to the "grace tree" and talk about some practical ways to feast on the fruit of the tree of life.

Chapter 12
Eating From the Tree of Life

I would like to spend some time exploring a few ways we can eat from the tree of life. As we have discussed, apart from the Genesis accounts, this tree is mentioned only a few times in the Bible—in Proverbs and also in Revelation. Although these references are figurative, they still give insight into our freedom. However, before we look at these verses, we are going to study one other way to partake of this fruit: through the act of taking Communion.

Like most concepts linked to grace, the accuser has been relentless in his distortion of this vital New Covenant activity. Many spiritual realities have a high degree of imaging associated with them. We talk

> *Communion is a hands-on, physical way to experience the life of heaven.*

about fixing our eyes on Jesus and abiding in His love, but

Communion is a hands-on, physical way to experience the
life of heaven. We are actually eating and drinking something, mirroring a natural, daily function that is essential in
order for us to stay alive.

Look, Take, and Eat

Let us go back to Eden, the garden of pleasure and
delight, and look at some language used in reference to eating
from a tree. We quoted this passage several chapters ago, but
now we are going to focus on a different part of it.

> *When the woman saw that the tree was good for food,*
> *and that it was a delight to the eyes, and that the tree was*
> *desirable to make one wise, she took from its fruit and ate;*
> *and she gave also to her husband with her, and he ate.*
> (Genesis 3:6)

What I would like us to notice here is how Eve first
looked at the tree, and then she took and ate. The wording is
very specific. We have already seen that had Adam and Eve
eaten from the tree of life, the process would have been the
same: looking, taking, and eating. Now let's go to the New
Testament and consider something Jesus said the night of His
betrayal, when He was celebrating the meal of the Passover
with His disciples.

While they were eating, Jesus took some bread, and after a blessing, He broke it and gave it to the disciples, and said, "Take, eat; this is My body." (Matthew 26:26)

Notice the nearly identical phrasing used here by Jesus. It has a familiar ring to it: take, and eat. In this passage, Jesus uses the same language to describe eating from the new tree of life. The fruit, to be specific, is

> *As we take and eat of His body and His blood, we are celebrating a brand new way of doing life.*

His broken body and His spilled blood. The Luke version of the Lord's Supper actually quotes Jesus as saying His blood is the "blood of the New Covenant" (Luke 22:20). This statement is very significant since we are now aware what the New Covenant is: the new law written on the inside of our hearts. As we take and eat of His body and His blood, we are celebrating a brand new way of doing life. We have been severed from the old Law and released into the freedom of love, written invisibly with His blood.

There have been many doctrines and ideas surrounding the Lord's Supper over the years, and there is much mystery involved in this sacred meal. Some claim that the Communion elements literally become Jesus' blood and body. This transubstantiation is done via a miracle when prayed over by the clergy. Other denominations won't allow Communion to be taken by an individual who is not part of their religious belief system. Still others require certain regulations to be met. And the list goes on. Not many people realize that this event is a fulfillment of the Old Testament Passover feast. There are literally dozens of types and foreshadows which could be explored here, however, for the most part we are going to stay with the New Testament account of Communion and focus on the gift of life it offers.

The Sermon that Emptied the Street Corner

Let us start with Jesus' own words. He had just fed the 5000, walked on the water, and many people were duly impressed. They started questioning Him about manna and asking Him to show them another sign from heaven. In the Gospel of John it states that they were planning to take Him by force and make Him king. At this point in time He was at the pinnacle of His public ministry, but it always amazes me how Jesus didn't feel the need to capitalize on momentum here. Most of us in the same position would have grabbed the opportunity to put together a massive, world-winning evangelistic campaign. So what did our Master do? He preached a sermon so offensive and vulgar that all of His followers left except for the twelve disciples. He then turned to them and asked, "Do you want to leave as well?" They looked at Him and replied, "Lord, to whom shall we go? You have words of eternal life." (John 6:66-68) Here is some of the content of this PG rated sermon:

> So Jesus said to them, "truly, truly, I say to you, unless you eat the flesh of the Son of Man and drink His blood, you have no life in yourselves. He who eats My flesh and drinks My blood has eternal life, and I will raise him up on the last day. For My flesh is true food, and My blood is true drink. He who eats My flesh and drinks My blood abides in Me and I in him. As the living Father sent Me, and I live because of the Father, so he who eats Me, he also will live because of me. This is the bread which came down out of heaven; not as the fathers ate and died; he who **eats** this bread will **live forever**." (John 6:53-56, emphasis mine)

Although this homily caused many to walk away, you have to admit, without a discerning heart, these remarks would have sounded pretty strange. Not too many people would hang around a street preacher insisting his listeners need to eat his flesh and drink his blood in order to live.

The Tree of Life – Accessible Once Again

Let's examine Jesus' words a bit closer. He states that if we eat of the bread of life (i.e., His flesh) we will not die but live forever. Let us compare this statement to a verse we quoted earlier:

> *Then the Lord God said, "behold, the man has become like one of Us, knowing good and evil; and now, he might stretch out his hand and **take** also from the tree of life, and **eat**, and **live forever.**"* (Genesis 3:22, emphasis mine)

Notice the order of the words: stretch out your hand, take, and eat. Also, take note of what the tree of life does: it causes those who eat from it to live forever. Now, let us turn back to John. Jesus is talking about eating His flesh and drinking His blood. This passage is a direct symbolic reference to the Lord's Supper, but it is also a reference to the tree of life: they are one and the same. If the reincarnated tree of life is the crucified Jesus on the cross; then the fruit of this tree would be the His broken body and blood. If you recall, in the beginning God had to remove access to the tree of life from Adam and Eve in order to keep them from living forever in a fallen state. But now through the cross, and subsequently the act of taking Communion, we have been given direct,

> *I*f the reincarnated tree of life is the crucified Jesus on the cross; then the fruit of this tree would be the His broken body and blood.

physical access to this fruit again. Never underestimate the power of this fruit. It is just as saturated with the glory, life, and presence of God as it was back in the garden. Next time you partake of this meal, think of the fact that you are eating from the tree of life. Think of all of the things that the tree of life did back in the garden, or, if you like, look at the last chapter of Revelation.

> *Then he showed me a river of the water of life, clear as crystal, coming from the throne of God and of the Lamb, in the middle of its street. On either side of the river was the tree of life, bearing twelve kinds of fruit, yielding its fruit every month; and the leaves of the tree were for the healing of the nations.* (Revelation 22:1-2)

Here we see a picture of this tree. Evidently it grows different crops of fruit, which have regenerating and healing powers. In this New Covenant meal we have been given everything that pertains to life and godliness (2 Peter 1:3). In John's narrative, everything Jesus says has hidden meaning. He talks about abiding, stating that if we eat and drink His flesh and blood, we take up residence with Him and He with us. This act of partaking is part of the process of abiding in His love. Jesus also mentions gaining eternal life and living forever, all things that are possible if we would eat and drink this fruit of life.

There are few who approach Communion in this way. We understand that it is a celebration of the cross, but we do not understand that we are eating and drinking the very life of heaven. When we eat the Lord's Supper, we are indeed eating from the new tree of life: the cross. It is a meal of grace released from the wounds of Jesus. It is interesting that we are to eat and drink in remembrance of Him. First, we stretch out our hand or, in other words, look. Looking is the remembering part: we gaze at the cross, and in this gaze we reach out to him. It is important for us to fix our eyes on Jesus: He is the bread of life. Then we take, and eat.

Taking

Let's explore the idea of "taking" for a moment. A few chapters ago we talked about faith and how it activates grace. Think about the act of taking a piece of fruit from a tree. Now, in the same way, think of something made available at the cross such as "peace" or "healing." In order to appropriate it in our life, we first need to believe it is for us; requiring faith. This act of believing, takes the fruit of our redemption from the cross, in turn releasing the empowerment of grace to bring it from the heavenly realm onto this earth.

Now that we have talked about some of the practical aspects of the fruit of life, let us turn our attention to what it has changed into throughout the years. In order to explore these thoughts, we will look at the revelation Paul was given into the Lord's Supper, found in 1 Corinthians 11. There is much confusion over this text. Some of it is over the context in which it is written, other parts have subtleties contained in certain Greek words that are difficult to translate, leaving us with some very conflicting thoughts. We are going to try to unravel some of this mystery because it is vitally important to the way we celebrate this feast of love.

The Lord's Supper Gone Wrong

Let's begin with the context. The Corinthian Christians were doing some things terribly wrong when it came to celebrating the Lord's Supper, and Paul was writing to try and correct them. He makes an initial reference to Communion in chapter 10:

> *Is not the cup of blessing which we bless a sharing in the blood of Christ? Is not the bread which we break a sharing in the body of Christ? Since there is one bread, we who are many are one body; for we all partake of the one bread.* (1 Corinthians 10:16-17)

Paul is talking about how when we break a loaf and eat from it, or share the cup together, it represents the fact that while there are many of us in the body of Christ, we are all one. Then, in the next chapter, he references Communion again:

*For in the first place, when you come together as a church,
I hear that divisions exist among you; and in part I believe
it. ... Therefore when you meet together, it is not to eat the
Lord's Supper, for in your eating each one takes his own
supper first; and one is hungry and another is drunk.
What! Do you not have houses in which to eat and drink?
Or do you despise the church of God and shame those who
have nothing? Which shall I say to you? Shall I praise you?
In this I will not praise you.* (1 Corinthians 11:18, 20-22)

Immediately Paul starts talking about the divisions
among the members of this church. In the context of the
Lord's Supper, he is not happy because part of Communion
symbolizes us being one body—in other words, no divisions.
He then gives a glimpse into some of the other things that
had been going on. Evidently in the Corinthian gatherings
some would eat, others would go hungry, and some of them
would even get drunk. Paul seems particularly perturbed
that some would have plenty of food while others would
have nothing. These people had very little idea what the
Lord's Supper was about, and their gathering was destroying
the basic Communion imagery of the body of Christ being
united, helping, and caring for one another. Then the veteran
apostle begins to teach the church what this act of sharing is
supposed to be about.

For I received from the Lord that which I also delivered to you, but that the Lord Jesus in the night in which He was betrayed took bread; and when He had given thanks, He broke it and said, "this is My body, which is for you; do this in remembrance of Me." In the same way He took the cup also after supper, saying, "this cup is the new covenant in My blood; do this, as often as you drink it, in remembrance of Me." For as often as you eat this bread and drink the cup, you proclaim the Lord's death until He comes. (1 Corinthians 11:23-26)

Up until now, this passage sounds very much like the words Jesus used when He was sharing the Passover with His disciples. Notice again the cup represents the New Covenant, and it is written in His blood. Also, we are to share this meal in remembrance of Him, or while thinking about Him. But here is where the translation gets challenging. If the next few verses are translated with a "law" bias, our Communion theology can quickly go places where grace cannot reach. I have been at multiple Communion services in my life. What often happens is that the host tells people to look inward, examine themselves, and try to find hidden sin. Then, they are told to repent of that sin in order to avoid eating condemnation or judgment on themselves.

First of all, if we are thinking about ourselves during the Communion meal, how can we be fixing our eyes on Jesus at the same time? In focusing on ourselves, we are eating from the tree of knowledge of good and evil rather than the tree of life. I believe, for the most part, Satan has taken the Lord's Supper and reoriented it from what it was meant to be, a sharing in the tree of life, toward the exact opposite goal, a community sharing in the tree of the knowledge of good and evil. As a result, death is being released to the people of God through the act of taking Communion rather than the intended life. For this reason we are going to look at the next few verses in this narrative carefully, sometimes even one word at a time.

> *In focusing on ourselves, we are eating from the tree of knowledge of good and evil rather than the tree of life.*

*For whoever eats the bread or drinks the cup of the Lord in an **unworthy manner**, shall be guilty of the body and the blood of the Lord.* (1 Corinthians 11:27, emphasis mine)

The Greek word translated here as "an unworthy manner" is "anaxios." It is an adverb used only twice in the New Testament and it is subtly difficult to render into the English language. Since we have been made entirely worthy through Jesus' work on the cross, one defendable interpretation of this word is having an "unworthy mindset," rather than being unworthy because of sin we might have committed. In fact, another recognized rendering of "anaxios" is "unworthily." Let us look at the same verse in the King James Version.

> *Wherefore whosoever shall eat this bread, and drink this cup of the Lord, **unworthily**, shall be guilty of the body and blood of the Lord.* (1 Corinthians 11:27 KJV, emphasis mine)

If we come into the presence of the Lord feeling unworthy, where do we have our eyes focused? I can tell you exactly where they are focused: on ourselves. What we are doing is seeing nakedness, which is making us feel unworthy. Subsequently, we are approaching the Lord's Supper "unworthily," or with an unworthy mindset. In this position we become guilty of the body and blood of Jesus because we are trying to purge ourselves of sin in His presence rather than steadfastly fixing our eyes upon, and remembering Him.

Never enter the presence of the Lord feeling unworthy, especially at Communion time. This negative emotional posture is the exact opposite of the way He wants us to come to the cross and His table of blessing. We should be coming "in Him," knowing that by His blood we have been cleansed and made fully worthy. In turn, we can have confidence before the throne of grace. Let us read on:

*But a man must examine himself, and in so doing he is to eat of the bread and drink of the cup. For he who eats and drinks, eats and drinks **judgment** to himself if he does not **judge** the **body** rightly.* (1 Corinthians 11:28-29, emphasis mine)

These two verses need to be read together in order to catch their full context and meaning. Let us start with the second sentence. The word translated "judgment" here is the Greek word "krima." It can be translated as "condemnation" or "judgement." It means that we have been tried by the law, judged guilty, and condemned to damnation or punishment. Then, the word translated as "judge" used in reference to the body is the Greek word "diakrino." It can also be translated "discern" or "decide." This word speaks of thinking something "through" and coming to a conclusion or a determination. There is one more discrepancy to clear up before we go on. The "body" being referred to here in the Greek text is specifically the "body of the Lord"—the "soma" (body) of "kurios" (Lord, Master, Sir).

Let's put all of these concepts together. We are told to examine ourselves (take a close look at the state of mind and heart we are in) because, while taking Communion, we are in danger of being judged and condemned if we do not correctly discern (or come to a right determination of) the body of the Lord. The question is: what would be involved in discerning the body of the Lord wrongly? We have already talked about this subject quite extensively, but let's review the ideas again in the context of Communion. The body of Jesus was given as a sacrifice. He came in the likeness of sinful flesh, and on the cross took the sin-nature that was in our bodies into His pure body. He then died and condemned sin in the flesh. Remember, when He was crucified we were present "in Him" ("I have been crucified with Christ; and it is no longer I who live, but Christ lives in me," Galatians 2:20). Because of what He has done, we are now free from the sin-nature. If we go to the Communion table thinking that we still have an old sin-nature, looking for hidden sin, and feeling unworthy

> *If we go to the Communion table thinking that we still have an old sin-nature, looking for hidden sin, and feeling unworthy because of it, we are discerning the body of Christ wrongly.*

because of it, we are discerning the body of Christ wrongly. In this condition we are under the Law instead of under grace, and we are judged by the Law. Paul is urging us here to examine our hearts to make sure that we are approaching the Lord's Supper under grace rather than under law. It is, in fact, very dangerous to approach Communion from a law standpoint. If you don't believe me, consider the next verse:

> *For this reason many among you are weak and sick, and a number sleep* [i.e., many have died prematurely]. (1 Corinthians 11:30)

Think about it for a moment. What produces death? Law produces sin, which produces death (1 Corinthians 15:56). It has been this way since the beginning of time. There is one more verse to look at here:

> *But if we judged ourselves rightly, we would not be judged.* (1 Corinthians 11:31, emphasis mine)

Once more, let us consider a few Greek translations. The first word "judged" is the Greek word "diakrino," which we previously discussed and translated "discern" or "decide." Also, keep in mind that if you carefully study the context of this verse, it is still referring back to judging or discerning the body of the Lord rightly. The second word "judged" is the Greek word "krino." It means a judge has deliberated a case, and then made a decision or determination to condemn, punish, damn, or sentence by law. So, in other words, if we would correctly discern for ourselves the body of the Lord, we would not be judged or condemned by the Law.

In the last couple of verses in this chapter, Paul returns to the idea of eating at home before coming to a Communion celebration. That way, when we come together for the Lord's Supper, we don't have a situation where some are eating to the point of gluttony while others go hungry, which Paul states can bring judgment as well.

Personal Revelation

I distinctly remember the moment a few years ago in which I received a revelation concerning the Lord's Supper. I was meditating on the writings of Paul we have been studying and suddenly, for the first time in my life, I caught a glimpse of Communion the grace way. Then, just as suddenly, another thought hit me: all of my life I had been eating and drinking judgment on myself because I was approaching Communion with a sin-conscious, unworthy mindset. I was taught this method from an early age, and had no idea what I was doing. I cannot adequately express to you the grief of that moment. I cried my eyes out for at least twenty minutes straight. I was not weeping for myself alone; my heart was broken for the body of Christ at large, and I began to feel the grief of the Holy Spirit over the Communion feast. Most of the time, we come to this table, week after week, bringing an exact opposite mindset to what we should be bringing. Through my tears I recalled a recent Sunday during which our pastor had asked the congregation how many needed a touch of healing in their bodies. I watched as well over 70 percent of the people put their hands up. This reality also hit me hard as the phrase, "for this reason many among you are weak and sick, and a number sleep" began cycling over and over in my mind (1 Corinthians 11:30).

The problem is that we still think we have a sin-nature, and so we discern the body of the Lord wrongly. In the act of taking Communion, we repeatedly eat and drink condemnation on ourselves. Satan is indeed a killer, and he has twisted the meaning of this beautiful, life giving tree and its fruit around to deceive us again into eating from the tree of the knowledge of good and evil. This ruse was his plan in the garden from the start and it hasn't changed. He has no original ideas.

The Lord's Gracious Supper

Now, let's go through the process of taking Communion the grace way. First of all, there is a small phrase in Matthew I would like to quote:

Give us this day our daily bread. (Matthew 6:11)

Hardly a day goes by when I don't take Communion, and the reason is more than merely trying to make up for lost time. I find the tree of life has a cumulative effect on me. The glory of this fruit builds up over weeks and months, and recharges me with the life of heaven. Often my wife and I will take Communion together, sometimes a few times a week depending on our schedules. Here is what I do personally when I come to the Lord's Table. I am not saying the following description is the only way; it's just what works for me. First, I thank Jesus for His most remarkable gift of grace to me. I give Him thanks for neutralizing my old sin-nature and making me a brand new person—spirit, soul, and body. I then focus my eyes on Him, stretch out my hand, take by faith everything He has given me through the cross, and eat from the tree of life. It doesn't matter if I am celebrating this grace-meal on my own or in a corporate setting; I always do the same thing. I refuse to listen to any Communion exhortation that tells me to look at myself. If I inadvertently find myself in

> *From the beginning, Communion was meant to be an encounter with Jesus, who is the life of the world.*

this type of situation, I tune that message out and purposefully fix my eyes on Jesus instead.

I have determined that I will never again eat and drink condemnation and death on myself. Instead, life is being released into me with each and every Communion encounter. I use the word "encounter" deliberately because, from the beginning, Communion was meant to be an encounter with Jesus, who is the life of the world. In these simple actions I have discovered a world of life, healing, glory, and regeneration.

Wisdom and Righteousness

Now, as promised, let us talk about the other references to the tree of life in the Bible. We will start in Proverbs, where Solomon is talking about wisdom:

> *She is a tree of life to all those who take hold of her, and happy are all who hold her fast.* (Proverbs 3:18)

> *The fruit of righteousness is a tree of life.* (Proverbs 11:30a)

The first two things mentioned by Solomon that have to do with the tree of life are personifications of Jesus. There is one verse in the New Testament that covers both of these fruits of the tree of life:

> *But by His doing you are in Christ Jesus, who became to us wisdom from God, and righteousness and sanctification, and redemption.* (1 Corinthians 1:30)

Here we see Jesus has become both wisdom and righteousness to those who are found "in Him." It is not surprising, then, that these two redemptive qualities are referenced in context with the tree of life. Jesus hanging on the cross became the personification of the tree of life for us. As we fix our gaze on Him, we are transformed into who He is. I want to point out the feminine aspect of wisdom in the above reference. God is the perfect combination of both feminine and masculine attributes (Genesis 1:26-27), and it is interesting to note that throughout the book of Proverbs, wisdom is given a feminine personification. It is important that we do not think of wisdom as a substance or commodity. It is easy to seek after wisdom as a good thing to be had rather than seeking after a person to be encountered (i.e., Jesus). In one case it is knowledge, and in the other it is a relationship. The same is true for righteousness. Our right-standing with God is due to the fact that we are in Him, which again requires a relationship.

> *It is easy to seek after wisdom as a good thing to be had rather than seeking after a person to be encountered.*

Fulfilled Desire

Here is another reference to the tree of life:

> *Hope deferred makes the heart sick, but desire fulfilled is a tree of life.* (Proverbs 13:12)

I could talk about desire all day and night. Because I am a dreamer, it is one of my favorite subjects. I love scripture verses that speak of the desires of our heart, and there are many of them we could look at. One thing that has always amazed me about God is how our desires matter to Him. It seems like the moment when we have laid down our lives and wills on the altar of submission, our heavenly Father turns to us and says, "So now what do *you* desire?" He has never wanted robots, and, as I mentioned before, He is not a control freak. Even His will is not a method by which He can control us, as many of us think. Instead, it is a place where we are free to be who we really are. There are entire volumes that could be written on this subject, but we will leave it for another time. Here is one of my favorite "desire" scriptures:

> *Trust in the Lord and do good; dwell in the land and culti-*
> *vate (feed on His) faithfulness. Delight yourself in the Lord;*
> *and He will give you the* **desires** *of your heart. Commit*
> *your way to the Lord, trust also in Him, and He will do it.*
> (Psalm 37:3-5, emphasis mine)

There are at least two ways this scripture can be interpreted, and I believe both of them contain vital truths. First, the Lord actually places desires into our hearts. When each one of us was born, God put in us the seeds of life and destiny. As we delight ourselves in Him, these seeds are watered and dormant desires begin to spring to life, fueled by the destiny God has deposited in us. Second, once these desires are awakened by His love and we commit our way to Him in trust, He brings them into fulfillment in our lives. The most mysterious and delightful part of this process is: our heavenly Father is so good, He lets us think these desires were our idea right from the start. In a way they are, yet they proceed straight from His omnipotent heart in a way that gives us dignity and fulfillment in life. What an amazing heavenly Father we have! Here is another "desire" passage:

> *O my soul, bless God, don't forget a single blessing! He forgives your sins—every one. He heals your diseases—every one. Who redeems your life from the pit and crowns you with love and compassion, who satisfies your **desires** with good things so that your youth is renewed like the eagle's.* (Psalm 103:2-5, NIV, emphasis mine)

Our heavenly Father is so good, He lets us think the desires of our heart were our idea right from the start.

Here we see that our Lord satisfies our desires with good things. A direct benefit of fulfilled desire is that our youth is renewed like an eagle's. There are many ancient myths about the eagle and how its youth is renewed. Some of them focus on the natural molting process an eagle goes through as it ages. Others are much more sensational. One legend, cited in numerous ancient Christian writings, claims an aging eagle will fly towards the sun, get its feathers scorched by the heat, plunge into a lake three times, and come out with a brand new lease on life. Although factually suspect, I suppose with a bounteous imagination, it could paint a pretty sweet picture of us flying toward the glory, being changed into His image, and, well, possibly being baptized three times—once for each member of the Trinity!

It is interesting that fulfilled desire can have a "renewed-youth" effect on us. This passage is saying much the same thing, "desire realized is a tree of life" (Proverbs 13:12). Eating from the tree of life renews and energizes us. Maybe the "fountain of youth" is not such a myth after all!

A Soothing Tongue

Here is another Proverbs reference:

> *A soothing tongue is a tree of life, but perversion in it crushes the spirit.* (Proverbs 15:4)

Words can carry the life of heaven in them. The first few verses of John state that the Word of God came down from heaven, and in Him was life. As already mentioned, an encounter with Jesus is an encounter with the living Word. If we are abiding in Him, He then abides inside of us as the "Word." We need to be sensitive to the people around us, releasing His life to them through our words. I am not merely talking about saying nice things to people; I am talking about allowing Jesus to express His heart to them through us. There is a subtle difference between saying something nicely and saying something with "spirit and life." Listen to what our Savior had to say about this subject:

> It is the Spirit who gives life; the flesh profits nothing; the words that I have spoken to you are spirit and life. (John 6:63)

I have noticed in my own experience that a single phrase can be repeated twice: one time releasing nothing but natural energy, and the second time releasing the life of heaven. Think for a moment about a simple statement such as, "Bless you!" It can be blurted out habitually after a sneeze, or it can be released as a prophetic declaration over a person, carrying with it the very

We can only release the life-giving intentions of heaven if we perceive the heart of Jesus concerning the situations and people we encounter.

life, destiny, and grace of heaven. Although this example is over exaggerated, there are many subtle scenarios of this kind that happen to us on a daily basis. We can only release the life-giving intentions of heaven if we perceive the heart of Jesus concerning the situations and people we encounter. We then speak, dispatching words that are wrapped with life and charged with the anointing of the Holy Spirit, bringing hope, change and transformation.

Notice how it says that perversion, when released in words, crushes the spirit. Any time a word is spoken that doesn't broker the presence of heaven, it carries with it a certain amount of perversion. In this context, a crushed spirit is the opposite effect of the tree of life.

Access to Paradise

Now let's turn to the New Testament and the book of Revelation. Here we find the Apostle John, stranded on the island of Patmos, praying "in the Spirit on the Lord's day" (Revelation 1:9). Jesus appears to him and gives him messages for the seven churches scattered across Asia at the time. The first church addressed was the one in Ephesus. If you will recall, this church had left its first love. In His admonition, Jesus urges them to remember what their roots were, repent, and do what they did at first (Revelation 2:1-6). Here we see a reference to repentance. I want to recall once again the New Testament meaning of repentance: a change in thinking and direction that comes when we turn ourselves toward God, allowing us to be changed in His presence. It is a renewing of the mind. One of the surest ways to revitalize waning love is through a face-to-face encounter with the one we love. If we would simply fix our eyes on Jesus, the "Lover of our soul," we would quickly fall in love with Him all over again. He is, indeed, the desire of the nations. Continuing in the Revelation narrative, and the context of a renewed first love, we now find an exceptional verse:

> *He who has an ear, let him hear what the Spirit says to the churches. To him who overcomes, I will grant to eat of the tree of life which is in the Paradise of God.* (Revelation 2:7)

This reference to the tree of life is significant in that it was spoken to a church very much alive on the earth. However, notice where the tree is: it is in Paradise, or, in other words, heaven. To recap, a church alive and active on the earth is promised access to a tree in heaven. There is a similar phrase in a rather famous prayer Jesus taught His disciples:

> *Your kingdom come. Your will be done,* **On earth as it is in heaven.** (Matthew 6:10, emphasis mine)

We have been given an open invitation to heavenly realms through grace. If you recall a few chapters ago, we talked about the prayer life of Jesus; how He would access realms of glory, ascending and descending into spiritual places as he would pray. On one occasion, He allowed Peter, John, and James a window into this realm, taking them up to a mountain as He prayed and was transfigured before their eyes (Luke 9:28–29). To Jesus, prayer was an encounter with the very glory and atmosphere of heaven.

> *We have been given an open invitation to heavenly realms through grace.*

Here is another passage that describes a second experience John had with the glory of Paradise immediately after receiving the messages for the seven churches:

> *After these things, and behold, a door standing open in heaven, and the first voice which I had heard, like the sound of a trumpet speaking with me, said, "**Come up here**, and I will show you what must take place after these things." Immediately, I was in the Spirit; and behold, a throne was standing in heaven, and One sitting on the throne.* (Revelation 4:1-2, emphasis mine)

Here John, still praying in the Spirit on the Lord's day, was summoned to an encounter in heaven where he experienced heavenly worship, saw the throne of God, and witnessed things beyond comprehension. I suggest that the exceptional call, "Come up here," has been extended to each and every one of us. If this invitation were not for today, how else could we have been instructed to "draw near with confidence to the throne of grace" (Hebrews: 4:16)? I am, once again, stirring your heart to pursue a quest; a journey of discovery and encounter with this heavenly atmosphere. In this place of glory, you will find the tree of life.

In the next chapter we will discuss some practical aspects of grace. We will look at some scripture references that tell us where we can find it, and consider how it works to bring the exceptional realities of the cross into our lives.

Chapter 13
The Freedom of Grace

As He was setting out on a journey, a man ran up to Him and knelt before Him, and asked Him, "Good Teacher, what shall I do to inherit eternal life?" And Jesus said to him, "Why do you call Me good? No one is good except for God alone. You know the commandments, 'Do not murder, do not commit adultery, do not steal, do not bear false witness, do not defraud, honor your father and mother.'" And he said to Him, "Teacher, I have kept all these things from my youth up." Looking at him, Jesus felt a love for him and said to him, "One thing you lack: go and sell all you possess and give to the poor, and you will have treasure in heaven; and come, follow Me." (Mark 10:17-21)

To some, this narrative might represent a story about a rich young sultan with too much time on his hands, but to me, it is a story about grace. The scene opens up with a young man running towards Jesus, kneeling before Him in a posture of worship, and asking Him a very sincere question about inheriting eternal life. Being that he was a Jewish man under Mosaic Law, Jesus responded to him with a perfectly legitimate list of commandments that he should be keeping. The young man assured Jesus he had kept all these command-ments from the time he was a child. If we allow ourselves a window into the text, we can almost feel the desperation of this man. Even though he had been doing the right thing— keeping the Mosaic Law, there was still an emptiness in his life, a gnawing. He knew there must be something more and Jesus, no doubt, sensed the desperation of his heart.

At this point in time Jesus did three significant things. First He looked at him. If you have ever felt the eyes of the Master on your life, you will understand that it is impossible to catch the gaze of Jesus and remain unchanged. Second, Jesus felt love for him. Once again, when the love of Jesus penetrates our lives, it is difficult to return to normal. Third, Jesus spoke to him. Even though the clock of the ages was still set to "law," Jesus looked forward a few months in time to a brand new day—a day when grace would be released in all its fullness. He then reached into the future and pulled out a costly, yet mind boggling offer for this young man. It was an offer completely above law; it was an offer of grace: sell what you have, learn to give, and follow me—all of you for all of me. I might add that Jesus was not intending to drop this youthful proprietor off the edge of the boat. Instead, he was giving him the offer of a lifetime, an offer of love and freedom from law, an offer to spend time with Him and to get to know Him. The unique phrase, "follow me," was reserved exclusively for those called to be His disciples. Jesus was offering him a position on His staff. In this new context, there would have been little mention of the Law that so consumed the young ruler up to this point in time. Jesus would have enrolled him in the "Jesus Christ of Nazareth School of Grace" just as He did with the rest of His disciples.

> *The lifestyle of grace, at first glance, appears to have a hefty price-tag—it costs us everything.*

If we read on, we see this young man rejected Jesus' offer. The lifestyle of grace, at first glance, appears to have a hefty price-tag—it costs us everything, but in return we gain Jesus who is the essence of grace. In the end, those who choose to walk this road understand that any loss encountered pales in comparison to the freedom gained in an environment of grace.

Grow in Grace

These things being said, there is one vital point I would like to mention: grace is something we grow in. Here are a couple of scriptures:

> *But grow in the **grace** and knowledge of our Lord and Savior Jesus Christ.* (2 Peter 3:18, emphasis mine)

> *And Jesus kept increasing in wisdom and stature, and in **favor** with God and man.* (Luke 3:52, emphasis mine)

The word "favor" in the second verse is our word "charis." It is translated "grace" almost everywhere else in the New Testament. My point here is: if Jesus needed to grow in grace, we certainly do as well. The lifestyle of grace is a lifelong journey of discovery and surrender.

Grace Stations

As mentioned before, grace is an empowerment of divine favor and blessing, and in the New Testament its source is the cross. In other words, it is made available to us because of what Jesus did. The outflow of the cross reaches far and wide, all the way from the deepest parts of the earth to the throne room of God Himself. In the next few pages there will be four specific "grace stations" that we are going to highlight. These are places where grace can be found.

The Throne of Grace

The first one is in Hebrews 4, a chapter that is all about rest. Think back to the Garden of Eden and the lifestyle of rest that was enjoyed before the fall. Imagine walking among

THE FREEDOM OF GRACE

the trees in the cool of the day talking with Father God. Grace, faith, trust, and rest work side by side to bring about the realities of the cross in our life. The writer is talking here about our great high priest, Jesus. He states that Jesus is able to represent us before the throne because He lived here on earth, can sympathize with our weakness, and was tempted in all things just like us. It is here we find this classic verse:

> *Therefore let us draw near with confidence to the throne of grace, so that we may receive mercy and find grace to help in time of need.* (Hebrews 4:16)

Here we see that grace has stretched its hand right to the throne room of God. In fact, it has touched God's heart so deeply that He has given His throne a new name: it is now called the "throne of grace." If the preceding evidence

> **G**race has touched God's heart so deeply that He has given His throne a new name: it is now called the "throne of grace."

isn't enough to convince you of the importance of this New Testament empowerment, I don't know what else could. Grace is at the very center of the thoughts and intentions of heaven. John describes the ministry of Jesus as grace upon grace (John 1:16). There are also references in the Bible to grace being lavished upon us.

I encourage you: go before the throne of grace every day—and go boldly. In the presence of the glory is where you will find this grace. Anytime you have a need, grace is the answer. Hebrews 4:16 clearly states we find grace to help in "time of need." It doesn't matter what the need, grace is up to the task. Coming before the throne is an act of worship; and in the exchange that happens, we lay down who we are and then our Father gives us grace. Take this grace with you back to your place of need and release it. Speak it out loud! Consider what happened in the book of Zechariah:

> *Not by might not by power, but by My Spirit says the Lord of hosts. What are you, O great mountain? Before Zerubbabel you will become a plain; and he will bring forth the top stone with shouts of "Grace, grace to it!"* (Zechariah 4:6-7)

Here we see Zerubbabel, the prophet facing a mountain. He stands challenging the mountain, declaring it will become a flat plain before him. How does he accomplish this feat? He shouts, "Grace to it!" He is clearly releasing grace into the situation in order to get the job done by the Spirit of the Lord. If you have a problem, go to the throne, find grace, and then come back and speak the grace into the situation.

The Grace Saturated Words of Jesus

Now, here is a second place to find grace. This incident took place when Jesus first started His public ministry. He had just read a passage of Scripture in the synagogue which resulted in the following situation:

> *And all were speaking well of Him, and wondering at the gracious* [grace-filled] *words which were falling from His lips; and they were saying, "Is this not Joseph's son?"* (Luke 4:22)

The words of Jesus are grace-filled. In fact, they are so heavily saturated with grace, they fall from His lips. We are not going to talk again about the Word, as we have already discussed this subject a few times. Needless to say, an encounter with the Living Word is an encounter with grace. If you need grace, go to Him; listen to His words. His words are dripping with grace.

Our Words Release Grace

Now we will look at a third place to find grace. Every time the Apostle Paul opened one of his letters to a church he would release grace upon them. Let me give you an example:

> *Paul, an apostle of Christ Jesus by the will of God, to the saints who are at Ephesus and who are faithful in Christ*

> *Jesus:* **grace to you** *and peace from God our Father and the Lord Jesus Christ.* (Ephesians 1:1-2, emphasis mine)

He would do the same thing at the end of his letters. These gracious salutations were more than mere niceties to the saints in the churches. Paul, more than any other apostle, had a deep understanding of grace. He received a revelation of grace straight from Jesus Himself. When he would say, "Grace to you," he meant something specific. Paul was aware his words had power, and he used them deliberately. What I am suggesting is that *we* can release grace to people with our words. Consider this verse in Colossians:

> *Let your speech always be with grace, as though seasoned with salt, so that you will know how you should respond to each person.* (Colossians 4:6)

> *W*e can release grace to people with our words.

When we speak grace we are releasing the blessing, favor, and destiny of heaven to our brothers and sisters. In the environment of community, grace-filled words should flow from our hearts and through our lips to those around us. These life-giving proclamations create a culture of grace in which the empowerment of God can work.

Humility Releases Grace

Here is a fourth place where we can find grace, in the context of humility:

But He gives a greater grace. Therefore it says, "God is opposed to the proud, but gives grace to the humble." (James 4:6)

If we flip our Bible over just a few pages, Peter repeats nearly the same words, adding that we should clothe ourselves with humility (1 Peter 5:5). He then gives a definition of this humility:

Therefore humble yourselves under the mighty hand of God, that He might exalt you at the proper time, casting all your anxiety on Him, because He cares for you. (1 Peter 5:6-7)

It must be said here that true biblical humility is not thinking lowly of one's self. This mindset is actually false humility and it generates the opposite effect of pride in our lives. Instead, we humble ourselves by casting our anxiety on the Lord and by seeing ourselves as Jesus sees us.

We, as humans, were never built to shoulder care and worry. This burden is nothing more than fear of the future, and it is the greatest cause of stress and sickness in our lives.

When we bear this kind of anxiety, we are proudly saying that we are capable of taking care of things on our own rather than letting our heavenly Father care for us. In contrast, when we cast the care on Him, refusing to live under the burden, this passage refers to the resulting status as a place of humility. Here we must trust and rest, putting ourselves under the mighty hand of God, leaving the future with Him. In this environment we are given the amazing promise of "greater grace," a divine influence that will exalt us at the proper time and set us in heavenly places of blessing.

Gracious Realities

Now let us look at some of the things that are given to us through grace. If we continue in the narrative of Ephesians as quoted a few paragraphs ago, there are many blessings mentioned in reference to grace. When looking at these items, keep in mind that grace is not so much a commodity as it is a lifestyle free from law and rooted in the New Covenant. Let it also be mentioned that the grace of Christ is inexhaustible. Eternity itself will not be long enough for us to plumb the depths of this incredible gift. Therefore, this list of things touched by grace is only the tip of the iceberg. In the text we will be exegeting, everything relates back to this phrase: "to the praise of the glory of His grace, which He freely bestowed on us in the Beloved" (Ephesians 1:6).

We will now go through the narrative of Ephesians 1 verse by verse. These are my own paraphrases, but I encourage you to look this exceptional passage up when time permits.

Verse 2: Grace and peace are given to us from God our Father and the Lord Jesus Christ.

Verse 3: We have been blessed with every spiritual blessing in the heavenly places.

Verse 4: We have been chosen in Christ and made holy and blameless before Him.

Verse 5: We have been adopted as sons and daughters through Jesus Christ.

Verse 6: **To the praise of the glory of His grace,** which He freely bestowed on us in the Beloved. (emphasis mine)

Verses 7-8: We have redemption through the blood of Jesus and the forgiveness of sins, according to the riches of His grace which is lavished upon us.

Verse 9: He made known to us the mystery of His will; the kind intention of the Father toward us.

Verse 10: All things in heaven and earth are summed up in Christ, meaning that through grace we can make the declaration: "Let it be on earth as it is in heaven."

Verses 11-12: We have been given a glorious inheritance.

Verse 13: We have been sealed in Christ with the Holy Spirit of promise.

Then, in Ephesians 2, Paul states that we have been saved, raised up with Christ, seated with Him in heavenly places, and shown the riches of His kindness to us for eternity—all by grace (Ephesians 2:5-8). Our entire salvation past, present, and future flows out of grace!

Although we already have an impressive list of subjects touched by grace, there are more. Consider this verse in 2 Corinthians:

> *For you know the grace of our Lord Jesus Christ, that though He was rich, for your sake He became poor, so that you through His poverty might become rich.* (2 Corinthians 8:9)

Gracious Wealth

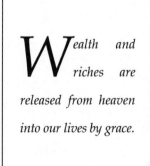

Wealth and riches are released from heaven into our lives by grace.

Here we see another work of grace. The context of these verses is speaking directly about money. In the financial realm, not many people realize that there are grace-filled pathways to discover. Wealth and riches are released from heaven into our lives by grace! I am going to say something a bit controversial here, and I beg you to not take the next few paragraphs in the wrong way.

There is a lot of talk right now about sowing financial seed and reaping harvest. I recently stayed in a hotel room in the Midwestern United States for a couple of days. Having a bit of time, I turned on the television and began to watch some Christian TV. Ministry after ministry came on appealing to people to sow financial seed, promising the bounty of heaven in return. After watching for a few hours on multiple channels, I was overwhelmed. I no longer wondered why my un-churched friends insist that preachers only want their money, even though I know perpetuating a negative image is not the heart of these ministries. I believe in the concept of sowing and reaping, and it is easy to find in Scripture; however, I would like to point us in a slightly different direction of thought.

Something given by grace cannot be worked for, and this notion includes sowing and reaping. The whole point of grace is: it is lavished on us freely and without agenda. I caution against taking any redemptive concept and attaching a "something put in equals something taken out" approach. For those with a law mindset, this kind of talk is nothing but candy to one's ears. We love to *work* for our salvation, but in the graciousness of Jesus we find the *finished work* of the cross.

For the subject of money, I would like to suggest that we endeavor to become "Spirit-led" in our giving and "grace oriented" in our receiving. By this statement I mean: we need to continually listen for the whispering of the Holy Spirit as He shows us the needs of our world, and then respond financially to those situations as He directs us. It might even do us well to strike the "sowing" idea from the equation for a while and give with no agenda except to love. On the other hand, our Father has extended to us an exceptional, open invitation. It is none other than to position ourselves daily at the throne of grace, where there is untold blessing and extravagance. Here we can boldly receive the bounty of heaven, and in this place of glory and rest we can declare with confidence, "May it be on earth as it is in heaven!" This kingdom pronouncement is not possible because of anything we have done, but because of everything Jesus has done, simply because we know our heavenly Father loves us!

Wow, what freedom and abundance there is in this approach! But it is not for the faint of heart. I want to remind you, as I have already stated, the requirement of grace is greater than the requirement of law. When it comes to our money, this thought can be frightening; however, the empowerment of grace is infinitely stronger than law. I will say it again: I believe in sowing and reaping when it comes to finances; however, I believe an even higher standard can be reached.

I see a day coming when people will both give and receive by this "grace" as seen in the scripture just quoted. In that day I see a Spirit-led generosity in the followers of Christ overflowing into an abundance of "grace finances" released among God's people. This overflow will be on a scale not known since the fourth chapter of Acts. I also see thousands of grace-filled ministries flourishing with untold plenty to the point where they will have to say, like Moses, "Stop, we have too much!" (Exodus 36:5-7). For those who would choose to eat from the tree of life in the area of finances, there is a selection of Scripture to which I would like to direct your attention:

> *Now a river flowed out of Eden to water the garden; and from there it divided and became four rivers. The name of the first is Pishon; it flows around the whole land of Havilah, where there is gold. The gold of that land is good; the bdellium and the onyx stone are there.* (Genesis 2:10-12)

This river has always baffled me, as it seems to run backwards. Most rivers start as many streams, which then flow together into one large river. This one is different. It starts as one river and then divides into four streams; but then again, life works the exact opposite of death. In the last chapter of Revelation, the river of life flows the same way. It has its source at the throne of God (the throne of grace) and proceeds from there, dividing to water all of heaven. In Eden, the first tributary, Pishon, flowed around a land bearing untold riches waiting to be gathered by those living in the garden environment. The word "Pishon" comes from a Hebrew root which means to grow fat, to spread out, and to be scattered. It seems from this example, it was part of God's original plan to spread His glory over the face of the earth—through the riches of the glory of His grace (Philippians 4:19). The fact this river is mentioned first in the Genesis account leads me to believe this subject is definitely a priority with God. I would like to suggest that for those abiding in Christ, this promise is certainly one to be claimed and prayed into. I can assure you, it is this way in heaven, and I invite you on a journey to encounter this grace given to us by our Lord Jesus Christ.

Gifts of Grace

There is another aspect of grace I would like to mention briefly. Every gift given to us by the Holy Spirit is given by grace. Let me illustrate with some scripture. Here Paul is talking about the gifts that were entrusted to him and, in specific, his apostolic calling:

> *To me, the very least of all saints, this grace was given, to preach to the Gentiles the unfathomable riches of Christ.* (Ephesians 3:8)

But to each one of us grace was given according to the measure of Christ's gift. And He gave some as apostles, and some as prophets, and some as evangelists, and some as pastors and teachers. (Ephesians 4:7, 11)

The ministry gifts we carry are given to us by and through grace. In other words, they are bestowed on us as a gift of grace; however, the power enabling us to effectively live them out is also a work of grace. Grace is not just the source of the five-fold ministries mentioned above, it is also the wellspring of every gift we use to serve one another and edify the body of Christ.

Strength in Weakness

There is one more scripture I would like to look at when it comes to the work of grace in our lives:

Because of the surpassing greatness of the revelations, for this reason, to keep me from exalting myself, there was given me a thorn in the flesh, a messenger of Satan to torment me—to keep me from exalting myself! Concerning this I implored the Lord three times that it might leave me. And He has said to me, "My grace is sufficient for you, for power is perfected in weakness." Most gladly, therefore, I will rather boast about my weaknesses, so that the power of Christ may dwell in me. Therefore I am well content

with weaknesses, with insults, with distresses, with perse-
cutions, with difficulties, for Christ's sake; for when I am
weak, then I am strong. (2 Corinthians 12:7-10)

These verses encompass the infamous passage about Paul's thorn in the flesh. There is a great deal of speculation over exactly what this thorn might have been. Some say it was an eye disease or some other kind of sickness. Others would refute this claim, saying it was a demonic force rather than a physical condition. From the context of these verses, it seems pretty clear to me it was a satanic assignment sent against Paul, following him everywhere he went, causing all the turmoil mentioned at the end of the reading; things such as insults, distress, and persecution. However, the point is the answer given by the Lord to Paul's dilemma: "My grace is sufficient for you, for power is perfected in weakness."

> *When Jesus told Paul that a walk of grace was the antidote to his problem, He wasn't merely giving him a pat on the back.*

I will ask you this question: what is your weakness, need, or problem? The answer is grace. When Jesus told Paul that a walk of grace was the antidote to his problem, He wasn't merely giving him a pat on the back. He was, instead, offering him all of the power of heaven to combat the condition of weakness he had been put in. At the end of his discourse, Paul was so excited to witness the power of grace in action, he actually said he was "glorying" in his weakness (2 Corinthians 12:9, KJV). The above scenario, as described by Paul, is a classic example of grace at work. When we are in our greatest condition of weakness, God's empowerment of grace is at its strongest. Once again, we can't work for it. We offer all we are in exchange for all He is—and who is He? He is love and grace personified! No matter what the condition, whether it is sickness, eye disease, or the nastiest demon hell has to offer, there is no power in heaven or on earth that can stand before the empowerment of the grace of our Lord Jesus Christ. The lifestyle of grace is the new reality of the resurrection side of the cross—freedom, salvation, rest, and victory.

In the next pages, we are going to return to the idea of revival and pursue what it might look like in a grace-impregnated personal and corporate environment.

Chapter 14
Grace upon Grace

Enter through the narrow gate; for the gate is wide and the way is broad that leads to destruction, and there are many who enter through it. For the gate is small and the way is narrow that leads to life, and there are few who find it. (Matthew 7:13-14)

In this last chapter I would like you to come on a journey with me. Once we pass through the gateway of grace, there is an exciting new road to follow, a tree to eat from that is saturated with life, and a pathway of freedom that

> *Once we pass through the gateway of grace, there is an exciting new road to follow, a tree to eat from that is saturated with life, and a pathway of freedom that few discover.*

few discover. It is a scandalous lifestyle—Jesus is offensively good beyond measure (Matthew 11:5-6). I would like us to dream together about this narrow way leading to life. As previously mentioned, dreaming is one of my favorite subjects. For the past few years, something has been building in the body of Christ—the Holy Spirit is beginning to re-emphasize grace. The reason I have written this book is because these gracious seeds have taken root in my heart and the hearts of many of my friends. This wave of God's Spirit started as a small spring with just a little trickle of water coming from it. However, it has been growing stronger with each passing year, and I think I would now classify it as a stream. There has been much opposition to this movement. I don't ever remember witnessing a more unrestricted public attack on a stream of thought as I have with this one. Because there is much at stake, we are going to look at a brief historical overview to see if we can discover where we have come from and where we are headed.

Let's start with the past. I have read much revival literature and there are excellent resources available for anyone who would choose to study this topic. The things I am about to say in the next few pages I intend with the utmost respect for those who have gone before, paving the way for the freedom we now have the privilege of walking in. The truth is, much has been lost to the Church through the ages. As far as I am aware, there hasn't been a generation yet that has walked in the same power and authority as the Church in Acts. I believe an honest review of this decline reveals one critical point of departure: we have inadvertently abandoned our Holy Spirit heritage (the heritage of being a people of His presence) in favor of religion. In my estimation, the cruelest aspect of religion is the simple fact that it doesn't recognize itself. The ultra-religious mastermind behind this scheme, the devil, has deceived us into substituting form for power, law for grace, to such an extent that we have become largely irrelevant on the face of the earth. Since the first century of the church age, there has been a slow and steady recovery of lost spiritual inheritance, but there is still much ground to be recaptured.

Pockets of Breakthrough

There have been pockets of breakthrough, life, and glory in different movements, but these have not lasted for long. Recently, I have been studying the great revival of the mid 1800's that took place in Hawaii. It started off with a great work, grew to include tens of thousands of souls, and then fizzled out within seven years. There are many others like it; some of them evangelistic in nature, others more spirit or healing focused, but all having the same premature end. Because of this cycle, most Christian leaders, intent on bringing revival to their cultural demographic, believe it is a sovereign move of God both started by Him and also stopped by Him. I have talked with many who believe there is a set expiry date of only a few years on any move of God.

Here is where we need to be ultra-respectful of the Spirit-led waves of the past. Just because a move of God had a glorious, life-giving atmosphere attached to it for a period of time, doesn't mean that all of the theology was correct, or that God was sanctioning the leadership. I have studied a lot of classic renewal theology. Most of us would agree in light of current revelation much of it was basic, and in some cases even quite wrong, but God blessed it anyway. So what was happening? The Holy Spirit was adding lost revelation back to the body of Christ bit by bit as they could handle it over time. Sadly, the theologies and lifestyles of the leaders would often bring the ministry down, and revival would stop way too soon. What God has been doing is honoring His word in spite of the human effort involved.

However, many renewals of the past were steeped in law. In the end they became about trying to live up to standards rather than beholding the face of Jesus, even though beholding Him is how most of these moves began. In the Hawaiian revival, the leaders actually went from village to village with a notebook keeping track of every person who had come to faith, calculating the amount of time each individual had put into prayer, and documenting whether or not they had been back to the local pub that week. Anyone found to have slipped up, had to make a severe penance of repentance.

This entire book has been about grace. It is easy to see there is no grace in this approach to salvation. If you take a group of people, and after initially getting them to put their eyes on Jesus, change their focus back to themselves, whatever glory they had will disappear quickly. In reading through similar accounts, wave after wave of God's movements have been administrated in the same way through the years.

> *If you take a group of people, and after initially getting them to put their eyes on Jesus, change their focus back to themselves, whatever glory they had will disappear quickly.*

I have come to one conclusion in the travels and experiences of my lifetime: God is infinitely more eager to display His glory on our planet than we have ever been to get Him to engage in our renewal efforts. However, in our religious fervor, we try many things in an attempt to coerce Him to act on our behalf, including varying amounts of prayer, fasting, and evangelism. We look back at past revivals to see if we can discover the key to their success—how much did they pray, how many tears did they cry over their city, did they fast, and what type of sermons were preached to inspire repentance? Here is where I tread with the greatest amount of respect.

I don't believe most of these moves of God started because of the things their founders were doing. I believe, in many cases, they started in spite of what they were doing, and simply because of their hunger for God. In the end, human nature took control, and these moves were truncated before their time. God might start revivals, sending the fire of His glory on the altar, but it is up to us to carefully steward those fires. We, God's people, have a horrendous track record in this regard. Here are a few simple, yet efficient revival killers I have noticed both in my lifetime, and in my studies on the subject:

- We throw cold waters of law and control on the revival fires.

- We try, with human effort, to capitalize on momentum outside of rest (this exploitation might even be with the best of motivations, such as saving the world).

- We take glory that should have been God's.

- We move away from the foundation of the revival (these cornerstones may be things we don't recognize as being foundational, such as worship).

- We try in some way to contain what we have rather than set it free.

God, in His desire to move, looks for people with hearts after His in spite of their theology, prayers, or tears. What He is seeking for are people who will worship Him in spirit and truth, focusing their eyes on Him with unquenchable hunger (John 4:23-24). Any group of people who will approach Him in this way, without agenda, will have the renewal they desire. A desperate heart, transformed by worship and grace, is something God can work with. I do not believe revival is rocket science, or that it is random. I don't believe it can be worked for, and I don't believe it happens by chance. Nor do I believe it needs to have a set expiry date, coming and going solely as a sovereign move of God. There is nothing that says it needs to start a certain way, or look like anything that has happened in the past. Down through the years, the concept of "revival" has evolved to encompass a lot of preconceived ideas. It is a word we have chosen to define the renewing effect of God's Spirit, but in my opinion, it doesn't even begin to describe the glorious waves of grace currently being released on our

> *A desperate heart, transformed by worship and grace, is something God can work with.*

planet. In fact, in some respects, the word "revival," along with its accompanying stereotypes, somewhat cheapens what the Spirit of God is doing across our world today. The body of Christ is in desperate need of new language to describe the way in which heaven is embracing our earth. We also need a paradigm shift in order to recognize and receive our Father's corporate touch of love and grace.

The Healing Revival

Now, let us take a quick look back through the decades and consider some of the most recent waves of the Spirit. We will choose the healing revival of the fifties and sixties as a place to jump into God's renewal timeline. The glory of this exceptional outpouring is well documented. I have sat, spellbound, as contemporaries of this move recited story after story of the miraculous atmosphere present in meetings and crusades. Countless healings took place while cities, towns, regions, and nations were changed and re-shaped forever.

Charismatic Kindness

Once this great revival began to wane, it gave way in the seventies to the "charismatic" movement. As a youngster I remember this shift well, it being my first introduction to the Holy Spirit. Growing up in a tiny farming community, our family hung out with a group of charismatic Catholics after being expelled from a more evangelistic church for speaking in tongues. Even though these dear people had an entirely different denominational view of God than we did, they were exceedingly kind, taking us in as if we were their own. I will remember and cherish their love, compassion, and friendship for the rest of my life.

Word of Faith

Then I witnessed firsthand the "word faith" movement of the eighties and nineties. I have attended many awe-inspiring meetings of this persuasion, sometimes the glory of heaven being so strong, I could scarcely stand on my feet. However, eventually, this movement began to give way to a great renewal of the prophetic as well as worship. I might add that each one of these waves of the Spirit was denounced as false and heretical by those in the previous renewal.

This short walk through renewal history brings us to where we are today. I have heard it said that God adds something offensive to each new wave of His Spirit. He offends the mind in order to reveal the heart, laying bare our motivations and the depths of our desperation and hunger for Him. This element of offence often gets people so upset they miss what He is doing altogether. If

> God offends the mind in order to reveal the heart, laying bare our motivations and the depths of our desperation and hunger for Him.

this statement is true, then in my estimation, the element of offense that is being added to the current move is none other than grace. I believe it is this way for a reason. There is only one way our world will be truly impacted with the message of the cross: through grace. I believe this move will be the last great wave of God on our planet before the return of Jesus. In the beginning it all started with grace, rest, trust, glory, and relationship; and I believe it will end the same way. Rather than moving us towards a super-heightened state of revivalist spirituality, our heavenly Father is bringing us back to normality, back to where we should have been all along. He is leading us back to the garden once again.

The Bride

One evening a short while ago, I was meditating on the Song of Solomon. In the third chapter we find a royal wedding, and a few verses later the bridegroom is telling His bride, "You are altogether beautiful, my darling, and there is no blemish in you" (Song of Solomon 4:7). All of a sudden, on the screen of my heart, a picture hit me. I saw the Bride of Christ, and she was absolutely beautiful. The way Jesus looked at her was indescribable; infinitely more riveting than anything I have seen on this earth. Dressed in a spotless white garment, she was decked out in purity and holiness, adorned with the very glory of heaven. From what I could see on the surface, she appeared to be mature and free, steadfast in her love, and secure in her identity in Christ. It was a stunning image, and I was taking in the magnitude of this picture when the scene started to change. I watched with panic as the Bride haphazardly got up from where she was. At this point I somehow saw deeper and perceived that all the beauty was nothing but positional "theological theory" to her. She had no idea who she was, didn't really think she was beautiful, and didn't seem to notice the love with which Jesus looked at her.

What I then saw brought me to my knees with the greatest sadness I have ever felt. She bolted out into a field, white dress flowing behind her, and jumped right in the middle of a small swimming pool sized mud hole. She was not dirty before taking this muddy leap, but the thoughts in her own mind, along with the things other people said, assured her she was. For this reason she didn't feel in her heart that she was worthy to be clean, and so she jumped in the mud. Jesus was right there. He saw the whole thing happen, went into the mud, and pulled her out. He tried to reassure her that she was clean and beautiful in His eyes. He brought water, washed her, and cleaned her up again. She stood there for a while looking at Him, and then looked at herself again. Immediately she started to feel bad, and for a second time headed straight for the mud. This cycle happened a few times before the vision finally passed from my heart.

I didn't realize it at the time, but I was seeing the classic struggle between law and grace, slavery and freedom, and the two trees we have spent so much time talking about. You see, we are the Bride of Christ. When will we ever learn

> *The problem is not that the Church is stained and sin-ridden; it is that she does not know how beautiful she really is.*

to be who we really are—free and beautiful? The problem is not that the Church is stained and sin-ridden; it is that she does not know how beautiful she really is. It is going to take a tsunami of grace to break through what centuries of law and eating from the tree of the knowledge of good and evil has handed down to us. We will never touch our world with the reality of the kingdom until we are so drunk on grace that it can be smelled across the continents on our breath. Here is another passage in Song of Solomon:

> *He has brought me to his **banquet hall**, and his banner over me is love.* (Song of Solomon 2:4, emphasis mine)

The phrase translated "banquet hall" in the above verse is a rather tame translation. The Hebrew text is "bayith yayin," which is much more scandalous to our modern ears. I have inserted the literal meaning in the rendering below:

*He has brought me to his **house of wine**, and his banner over me is love.*

There is something interminably exciting starting to happen on the earth right now. I see the body of Christ beginning to fix her eyes on the one she loves: Jesus. She is starting to follow Him into the house of wine. As she does so, she is beholding His glory, encountering Him, receiving life, and being transformed into His image. This transformation is not so much a change in who she is, but a change in how she views herself in Christ. Once self-image is corrected, life-altering power is ignited quickly and effortlessly. The message of grace is the only thing that can affect this kind of transformation.

Time to Dream

I dream of a day when we will finally wake up and recognize who we are. I see a day coming when we will gather around the presence of our Father rather than an "order of service" we have constructed to occupy our time and ease our conscience apart from His power. I dream of a time when we will both personally and corporately wait in His presence without agenda and time restraint; when we will rest our eyes on Him and be transformed into His image. I see a day coming when fellowship, worship, and breaking bread will be the mainstay of our gatherings; a day when sermons, proclamations, and teachings proceed out of direct encounter with Jesus, carrying with them the power and demonstration of heaven's kingdom rather than knowledge (albeit good or evil). I dream of a time when we come with no plan other than to find His; when we stop the clock, waiting on His love to fill us before venturing out into the world to love those He has put in our way. I also see a day coming when we do great and mighty deeds out of nothing but rest, when we learn to ascend and descend into heavenly places of glory, and when we feast continually from the tree of life.

I see a day coming when grace is at the forefront of our minds; when we are empowered, blessed, and sent from the throne of grace. I dream of this present small stream becoming a river, dividing and flowing to the four corners of the earth, bringing life to everything it touches. I also see a day when we will kneel in the presence of our King and take Communion together, eating from the tree of life as one Body and one Bride; secure in who we are in Him, beautiful and white. I see a day coming when we are so transformed by glory, grace, and the renewing of our minds that we don't give sin a second thought; we have laid down our bodies as a sacrifice of worship, and we rest assured that our old natures have been crucified with Christ.

What we fix our eyes on grows within us. This ageless reality is the greatest mystery of grace. When our eyes are no longer focussed on ourselves but on Him, the new law of love can be lived out effortlessly. Only then will our cities, cultures, and nations be transformed from the inside out. In this life-giving environment, I dream of a day when the

> *What we fix our eyes on grows within us. This ageless reality is the greatest mystery of grace.*

Spirit of God hovers over our gatherings with glory not seen since the Garden of Eden. As we reach out to the heavens, the glory and fire of God will extend towards the earth, the cries of both worlds meeting in the middle to create a symphony of sound that will shake the nations. I see a day when our planet is re-energized with love, life, and grace as His kingdom comes near. I see signs, wonders, and miracles coming that will stun both us and the world. These marvels will represent both the power and mischievous nature of God, because sometimes the most effective way to be a father is to play with your kids.

So what will be the flavor of this new wave of grace? It will not look like anything we have seen before. It won't be neat and tidy; it will be unreligious and offensive. It will also be multi-generational, with no one age group or demographic highlighted above another. In the last days the Holy Spirit will be poured out on all flesh; sons and daughters, the working class, and the aged—all will have a significant role to play (Acts 1:17-18). It is my belief that the hurting, the sick, the broken, and our aging saints, some of them well past their prime years, will hold critical keys to this renewal. God delights in hiding the keys to our breakthrough in places we least expect, putting them in vessels that in our minds, have little to offer. He then requires us to honor these people in order for the keys to be released. To those with a law/works mindset, this model will be denounced as absolutely ridiculous. In fact, we don't have to look far to see the derision already happening before our eyes. The reason: worship, fellowship, the presence of God, and encounter-inspired proclamation will be at the heart of all activities, and everything will be done out of rest.

I dream of a day when freedom is preached rather than sin, and under this message repentance will seem way too easy. This declaration will also be denounced as false, but people will be truly free for the first time in their lives; transformed by God's glory rather than will power and self-discipline. And, when confronted with the true goodness of God, multitudes in our fallen world will gladly yield to the desire of their souls—a gracious Jesus. In the end, millions, possibly billions, will be ushered back into the kingdom, bypassing organized religion and law, releasing freedom and Garden of Eden conditions upon our planet once again.

I see no expiry date to this wave of God's Spirit. It will indeed usher in the return of Jesus; coming back for the girl of His dreams, the one He cannot resist, the Bride who has rediscovered who she is through grace. We have already been united with Him in His death, burial, and resurrection; but

> *When confronted with the true goodness of God, multitudes in our fallen world will gladly yield to the desire of their souls—a gracious Jesus.*

when He returns, we will be united with Him in His reappearing, closing out this era and ushering in eternity.

And so, with these thoughts, we have come full circle. The garden environment of grace is both the starting and ending place. Even now, as in the beginning, there are only two choices: a personal knowledge of good and evil, or an encounter with the grace-saturated tree of life. From which tree will you freely choose? Lift up your eyes, stretch out your hand, take, and eat.

About the Author

Dean Maerz was born and raised in a small farming community on the Alberta prairies. As a youth, his aptitude for music set him on the path to becoming an accomplished musician. Upon graduation from high school, he toured extensively across North America and overseas in musical groups, during which time he met his wife, Adeline. After returning home and attending Bible college, Dean served as a music pastor in central Canada for a period of time. Adeline and Dean then moved to Vancouver, BC, where Dean took more technical training and pursued a career in audio recording and teaching.

Dean, however, couldn't shake the call of God on his life. In 1998, while attending a worship night led by a local youth ministry, he had an encounter with God that changed his life. Over the next few months, his passions and dreams were reawakened in the presence of God, and his physical, emotional, and spiritual health were restored through worship.

Dean feels the compassion of God, is sensitive to the heartbeat of heaven, and is passionate about the presence of the Holy Spirit. He longs to see the Church understand the grace of God, become glorious and strong, and be released into its destiny! Dean and Adeline currently reside in the Fraser Valley of Vancouver, BC, where Dean serves in a local church and also speaks at various events.

For more information go to:

www.DeanMaerz.com

or,

www.thegracetree.com